Smith Wigglesworth

WHEN THE FIRE FELL

Living a Life that is Ablaze for God

Dr Michael H Yeager

DEDICATION

These Sermons, Teachings and Experiences from **Smith Wigglesworth** have been **MODERNIZED** for those who truly hunger and thirst after all that **God** has made available through the life, ministry, sufferings, death and resurrection of **Jesus Christ**. My prayer is that not only will your life be touched by these **divine Truths**, but you yourself will truly step in to that realm where all things are possible .**God** is not a respecter of people, what he did for **Smith Wigglesworth**, he desires to do for you and me. May you experience **Wonderful** transformation and divine healing.

These true stories and Sermons have been modernized in order to make them more understandable and descriptive in our modern vernacular. All of the Sermons have been compiled from many different articles, books, stories, sermons, and writings of Smith Wigglesworth. Some of these are laso taken from the internet! There are acknowledgments throughout this book to give credit to those who recorded the stories, and wrote them down for the increase and benefit of our personal faith. Jesus Christ is the same yesterday today and forever. What he did for these people he will do for you and me!

CONTENTS

EXHORTATION

Smith Wigglesworth: This Is the Place Where God Will Show up!

You must come to a place of ashes, a place of helplessness, a place of wholehearted surrender where you do not refer to yourself. You have no justification of your own in regard to anything. You are prepared to be slandered, to be despised by everybody. But because of His personality in you, He reserves you for Himself because you are godly, and He sets you on high because you have known His name (Ps. 91:14). He causes you to be the fruit of His loins and to bring forth His glory so that you will no longer rest in yourself. Your confidence will be in God. Ah, it is lovely. "The Lord is the Spirit; and where the Spirit of the Lord is, there is liberty" (2 Cor. 3:17).

Born June 10th, 1859
Died March 4th, 1947

***Notice: There will be some repetition in this book. Please do not be offended by this fact.**

Smith Wigglesworth, often referred to as 'the Apostle of Faith,' was one of the early pioneers of the Pentecostal revival that occurred a century ago.

Without human refinement and education he was able to tap into the infinite resources of God to bring divine grace to multitudes.

Thousands came to Christian faith in his meetings, hundreds were healed of serious illnesses and diseases as supernatural signs followed his ministry.

A deep intimacy with his heavenly Father and an unquestioning faith in God's Word brought spectacular results and provided an example for all true believers of the Gospel.

May this site stir your faith and deepen your vision for the glory of God in our generation.

CHAPTER ONE

Acts 2:2 And suddenly there came a sound from heaven as of a rushing mighty wind, and it filled all the house where they were sitting. 3 And there appeared unto them cloven tongues like as of FIRE, and it sat upon each of them. 4 And they were all filled with the Holy Ghost, and began to speak with other tongues, as the Spirit gave them utterance.

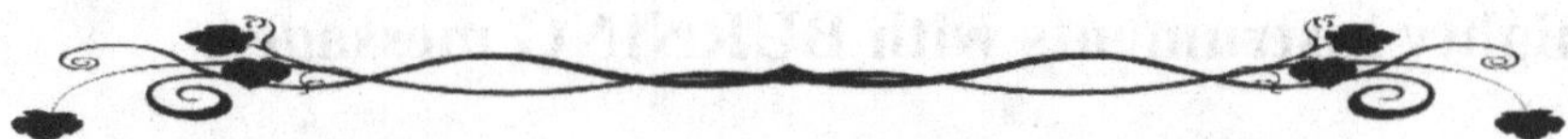

Smith Wigglesworth

*"Repeat in your heart often: "BAPTIZED with the Holy Ghost and FIRE, FIRE, FIRE!" All the unction, and weeping, and travailing comes through the baptism of FIRE, and I say to you and say to myself, purged and cleansed and filled with renewed spiritual power." "God Makes His Ministers a FLAME of FIRE" Heb. 1:7

*We must with our whole heart believe that the baptism of the **Holy Ghost** is meant to make us **FLAMES** of **FIRE**.

*John the Baptist said concerning Jesus, "He shall BAPTIZE you with the Holy Ghost, and with FIRE." God's ministers are to be a FLAME of FIRE—a perpetual FLAME, a constant FIRE, a continual burning FLAME, burning and shining lights. God has nothing less for us than to be FLAMES of FIRE.

We must have a living faith in God, a faith that God's great might and power may Burn in us until our whole life is energized by the power of God. *I see people from time to time very slack, cold, and indifferent; but after they get filled with the Holy Spirit, they become ablaze for God.

I believe that God's ministers are to be FLAMES of FIRE; nothing less than FLAMES; nothing less than mighty instruments with BURNING messages.

*I say all these things to you to move you into a living faith in **God**; for what will it profit me without some of you are turned into **FLAMES** of **FIRE**? What will it profit me if I turn from these meetings and you have only heard my voice and seen me? **God** would never have John and Peter and James to move up and down the world and leave people where they found them.

 *God wants to flow through you with measureless power of divine utterance and grace till your whole body is a FLAME of FIRE. God intends each soul in Pentecost to be a live wire. Not a monument, but a movement.

 *"If you want to increase in the life of **God**, then you must settle it in your heart that you will not at any time resist the **Holy Spirit**. The **Holy Ghost** and **FIRE** - the **FIRE** BURNING up everything that would impoverish and destroy you."

* I ask every one of you listening to the sound of my voice, will you hear the voice of God and come out? You ask, "What do you mean?" Everyone who is hungry for God knows without exception, there is only one word for Pentecost, and that is FIRE! If you are not on FIRE you are not in the place were God can mightily use you. It is only the FIRE of God that BURNs up the entanglements of the world.

*But oh, the BAPTISM in the **Holy Ghost**! The BAPTISM of **FIRE**! The BAPTISM of power! The BAPTISM of oneness! The BAPTISM of the association! The BAPTISM of communion! The BAPTISM of the Spirit of life which takes the man shakes him through, builds him up, and makes him know he is a new creature in the Spirit, worshipping **God** in the Spirit.

FIRE Fell After Receiving the HOLY GHOST

I was continually in those meetings causing disturbances until the people wished I had never come. They said that I was disturbing the whole conditions. But I was hungry and thirsty for **God**, and had gone to Sunderland because I heard that **God** was pouring out His Spirit in a new way. I heard that **God** had now visited His people, had manifested His power and that people were speaking in tongues as on the day of Pentecost.

When I got to this place I said, "I cannot understand this meeting. I have left a meeting in Bradford all on **FIRE** for **God**. The **FIRE** fell last night and we were all laid out under the power of **God**. I have come here for tongues, and I don't hear them-I don't hear anything."

"Oh!" they said, "when you get baptized with the **Holy Ghost** you will speak in tongues." "Oh, is that it?" said I, "when the presence of **God** came upon me, my tongue was loosened, and really I felt as I went in the open air to preach that I had a new tongue." "Ah no," they said, "that is not it." "What is it, then?" I asked. They said, "When you get baptized in the **Holy Ghost**-" "I am baptized," I interjected, "and there is no one here who can persuade me that I am not baptized." So I was up against them arid they were up against me.

I remember a man getting up and saying, "You know, brothers and sisters, I was here three weeks and then the **Lord** baptized me with the **Holy Ghost** and I began to speak with other tongues." I said, "Let us hear it. That's what I'm here for." But he would not talk in tongues.

I was doing what others are doing today, confusing the 12th of I Corinthians with the 2nd of Acts. These two chapters deal with different things, one with the gifts of the Spirit, and the other with the Baptism of the Spirit with the accompanying sign. I did not understand this and so I said to the man, "Let's hear you speak in tongues." But he could not. He had not received the "gift" of tongues, but the Baptism.

As the days passed I became more and more hungry. I had opposed the meetings so much, but the **Lord** was gracious, and I shall ever remember that last day-the day I was to leave. **God** was with me so much that last night. They were to have a meeting and I went, but I could not rest. I went to the Vicarage, and there in the library I said to Mrs. Boddy, "I cannot rest any longer, I must have these tongues." She replied, "Brother Wigglesworth, it is not the tongues you need but the Baptism. If you will allow **God** to baptize you, the other will be all right." "My dear sister, I know I am baptized," I said. "You know that I have to leave here at 4 o'clock. Please lay hands on me that I may receive the tongues."

She rose and laid her hands on me and the **FIRE**

fell. I said, "The **FIRE'S** falling." Then came a persistent knock at the door, and she had to go out. That was the best thing that could have happened, for I was ALONE WITH **GOD**. Then He gave me a revelation. Oh, it was wonderful! He showed me an empty cross and **Jesus** glorified.

I do thank **God** that the cross is empty, that Christ is no more on the cross. It was there that He bore the curse, for it is written, **"Cursed is everyone that hangeth on a tree."** He became sin for us that we might be made the righteousness of **God** in Him, and now, there He is in the glory. Then I saw that **God** had purified me. It seemed that **God** gave me a new vision, and I saw a perfect being within me with mouth open, saying, "Clean l Clean! Clean!" When I began to repeat it I found myself speaking in other tongues. The joy was so great that when I came to utter it my tongue failed, and I began to worship **God** in other tongues as the Spirit gave me utterance.

It was all as beautiful and peaceful as when **Jesus** said, "Peace, be still!" and the tranquility of that moment and the joy surpassed anything I had ever known up to that moment. But, Hallelujah l these days have grown with greater, mightier, more wonderful divine manifestations and power. That was but the beginning. There is no end to this kind of beginning. You will never get an end to the **Holy Ghost** till you are landed in the glory-till you are right in the presence of **God** forever. And even then we shall ever be conscious of His presence.

It was all as beautiful and peaceful as when **Jesus** said,

Smith Wigglesworth When the FIRE Fell

"Peace, be still!" and the tranquility of that moment and the joy surpassed anything I had ever known up to that moment. But, Hallelujah l have in these days I have grown with greater, mightier, more wonderful divine manifestations and power. That was but the beginning. There is no end to this kind of beginning. You will never get an end to the **Holy Ghost** till you leave this world into glory-till you are right in the presence of **God** forever. And even then we shall ever be conscious of His presence.

What had I received? I had received the Bible evidence. This Bible evidence is wonderful to me. I knew I had received the very evidence of the Spirit's incoming that the Apostles received on the day of Pentecost. I knew that everything I had up to that time was the anointing bringing me in line with **God** in preparation, but now I knew I had the Biblical Baptism in the Spirit. It had the backing of the Scriptures. You are always right when you have the backing of the Scriptures, and you are never right if you have not a foundation for your testimony in the Word of **God**.

For many years I have thrown out a challenge to any person who can prove to me that he has the Baptism without speaking in tongues as the Spirit gives utterance. It must be proved by the Word of **God** that he has been baptized in the **Holy Ghost** without the Bible evidence, but so far no one has accepted the challenge.

 I only say this because as many were as I was; they have a rigid idea that they have received the Baptism without the Bible evidence. The **Lord Jesus** wants those who preach the Word to have living the Word. Don't be misled by anything else. Have a Bible proof for all you have, and then you will be in a place where no man can deceive you.

At the time I received the Baptism in the Spirit, a meeting was going on in the large vestry of the All Saints' Church, and I went straight to it. The vicar of the church, Pastor Boddy, had charge and he was speaking. I knew that as yet he had not yet received the Baptism in the **Holy Ghost**, and I interrupted him by saying, "Oh, please let me speak, Mr. Boddy; I have just received the Baptism in the **Holy Ghost**."

The place was full of people. I can't remember what I said, but I know I made all those people extremely dissatisfied and discontented with their spiritual position. They said, "We have been rebuking this man because he was so intensely hungry, but he has come in for a few days and has received the Baptism and some of us have been waiting here for months and have not yet received." A great hunger came upon them all. From that day **God** began to pour out his Spirit until in a very short while 50 had received the Baptism.

The first thing I did was to telegraph to my home saying "I have received the Baptism in the **Holy Ghost** and have spoken in tongues."

On the train to my home town, the devil began questioning, "Are you going to take this to Bradford?"

Smith Wigglesworth When the FIRE Fell

As regards my feelings at the moment, I took no account of my feelings, for the just do not live by feelings but by faith. So I shouted out on the railroad coach to everybody's amazement, "Yes, I'm taking it!" A great joy filled me as I made this declaration, but somehow I knew that from that moment it would be a fight of Faith all the way.

When I arrived home one of my sons said to me, "**Father**, have you been speaking in tongues?"
I replied, "Yes, George."
"Then let's hear you," he said.

But I could say nothing, for although I had received the Baptism in the **Holy Ghost**, I had not yet received the distinct gift of tongues. That did not come until nine months later. My son did not understand that the speaking with tongues which accompanies the receiving of the Baptism in the Spirit is not the "gift of tongues" spoken of in 1 Corinthians 12. The former is given as evidence that the Spirit has come in Pentecostal fullness; but there may not be any further utterance in tongues unless there is a special anointing of the Spirit. The "gift of tongues," however, is such that the receiver may use it for prayer or praise at any time.

My wife said to me, "So you've been speaking with tongues, have you?" I replied, "Yes." - "Well," she said, "I want you to understand that I am as much baptized as you are and I don't speak in tongues."

I saw that the contest was beginning right at home.

"I have been preaching for 20 years," she continued, "and you have sat beside me on the platform, but this Sunday you will preach yourself, and I'll see what there is in it."

She kept her word. On Sunday she took a seat at the back of the building. We had always sat together on the platform until that day. So, the contest had begun right in the church.

There were three steps up to the platform and as I went up those three steps the **Lord** gave me the scripture in **Isaiah 61.1-3, "The Spirit of the LORD God is upon me; because the LORD hath anointed me to preach good tidings unto the meek; he hath sent me to bind up the brokenhearted, to proclaim liberty to the captives, and the opening of the prison to them that are bound." [Is 61.1-3]**

 I was no preacher but hearing the voice of my **Lord** speaking those words to me, I began. I cannot now remember what I said but my wife was terribly disturbed. ." I preached that night on the subject the **Lord** had given me and I told what the **Lord** had done for me. I told the people that I was going to have **God** in my life and I would gladly suffer a thousand deaths rather than forfeit this wonderful infilling that had come to me. My wife was very restless.

The bench on which she sat would seat nine people and

she moved about on it until she had sat on every part of it. She was moved in a new way and said:

 "That is not my Smith that is preaching. Lord, you have done something for him."

I was giving out the last hymn when the secretary of the mission stood up and said, "I want what our Smith has received." The strange thing was that when he was about to sit down he missed his seat and went right down on the floor.

There were soon fourteen of them on the floor, my own wife included. We did not know what to do, but the **Holy Ghost** got hold of the situation and the **FIRE** fell. A revival started and the crowds came. It was only the beginning of the flood-tide of blessing. We had touched the reservoir of the **Lord**'s life and power. Since that time the **Lord** has taken me to many different lands and I have witnessed many blessed outpourings of **God's Holy Spirit**.

Then my eldest son arose and said he wanted what his **Father** had and he, too, took his seat right down on the floor. The strangest thing was that they were all laughing in the Spirit and laughing at one another. The **Lord** had really turned again the captivity of Zion and the mouth of his children was being filled with laughter according to the word of the **Lord** in Psalm 126.1-2.

BEGINNING OF A GREAT OUTPOURING

That was the beginning of a great outpouring of the Spirit where hundreds received the Baptism in the **Holy Ghost** and every one of them spoke in tongues as the Spirit of **God** gave utterance.

God knew that I should have to go all over the world and proclaim this glorious truth, that all could receive the Baptism in the **Holy Ghost** in the same way as they received on the day of Pentecost with speaking in other tongues as the Spirit of **God** gives utterance.

The first call that I received after I had been baptized in the **Holy Spirit** was from a man who had a factory in Lancashire, and who employed more than 1,000 people. He wrote to say that he had heard that I had received the **Holy Spirit** as at the beginning, and he would like to meet a man who had received this experience. His letter said, "If you will come, I'll close down the factory each afternoon and give you five meetings between 1 p.m. and 11 p.m."

I wrote back, "I'm like a great big barrel that feels like bursting if it doesn't have a vent, so I'm coming to you for the meetings."

Up to that time I had no preaching abilities, but then I felt that I had a prophetic utterance which was flowing like a river by the power of the **Holy Spirit**. So I went to Lancashire; and that manufacturer closed his factory, and from 1 p.m. to 11 p.m., with short intervals, I was preaching. Surely Christ fulfilled his promise, **"He that believeth on me, as the scripture hath said, out of his belly shall flow rivers of living water."** [Jn 7.38] Quite a large number in that factory were gloriously saved.

Soon after this my dear wife received the Baptism in the Spirit and then we went forth together in response to the many calls that came from different parts of the country. Wherever we went the **Lord** baptized people with the **Holy Spirit**.

FIRE FELL AS POLLY PREACHED

We went together to a small place in Shropshire where we held a meeting in a Primitive Methodist Chapel. As my wife preached, the **FIRE** fell and people were baptized in the **Holy Spirit** all over that chapel. There was a good deal of opposition and plenty of persecution. It was a small country village and everyone around about seemed to be greatly moved. They all knew about that revival in that church.

The next morning after the "**FIRE** had fallen," I went walking around the village and entered a grocery shop. A deep conviction fell on three people who were in that shop and before I left that grocery store all three were saved. After I came out I went up the road a little and saw two women in a field who were carrying buckets. I shouted out to them, "Are you saved?" Here again a tremendous conviction seized them. They dropped their pails and began to pray; and right in that field the **Lord** saved those two women.

Wherever I went conviction seemed to be upon people. I went into a stone quarry where a whole lot of men were employed and I preached to them as they were dressing the big stones, and again conviction fell, and many were saved. As I was returning from this quarry, I passed a large hotel. Just as I was nearing it two men drove by in a two-wheel vehicle, and I never have seen men with such evil faces.

They looked the very picture of the devil. I did not know who they were but as they came near they began to cursed me and they tried to slash their whip at me. It seemed like an attack from the pit of hell. They shouted so loudly that the land**Lord** and landlady at the hotel and five people came out of that hotel and dashed at me like mad dogs, cursing and swearing, though I had not spoken a word to them.

But I did not fear their assault. I cried out instantly, **"In the name of Jesus, in the power of the blood of Jesus, I drive you back into your den."** They rushed back into the hotel and I went in and preached **Jesus** to them.

There were many people healed and baptized at that time and the glory of the **Lord** continued to fall. Twenty years later I visited that same village and the people recounted the story of that wonderful visitation from **God**. Many people from different parts of the country would come to our mission and on almost every occasion they would express the wish that I would visit their place and do something for them.

"

CHAPTER TWO

I had many telegrams to go to a place near Grantham to a young man who was very dangerously ill. After I arrived at Grantham I had nine miles to go by bicycle. When I came to that farmhouse that afternoon a woman at the door asked, "Are you Wigglesworth?" I replied, "Yes."

She said, "I am sorry to say that you are too late. My son is beyond anything being done for him now."

I answered, "**God** has never sent me anywhere too late."

I asked if I could see the young man. He lay in his bed with his face toward the wall and whispered that if he was turned over he would die, for his heart was so weak. "Well," I said, "I'll pray for the **Lord** to strengthen you."

In most of my work in those early days I used to pray much and fast. I knew that this case was beyond all human hopes and so I lay awake most of the night praying. I got up very early the next morning and went out to an adjoining field to pray, for I was very much burdened about this young man's situation. There in that field **God** gave me a revelation that this was a steppingstone in to a deeper realm in my life.

I went into the house and asked them to put their son's clothes to dry because the **Lord** would raise him up. In that part of England, the climate is very damp, so I knew it would be necessary for them to put his clothes before a **FIRE** before he could wear them. But they did not believe and so did not do anything about his clothes.

That was Sunday morning, and I knew that there was a service at the Primitive Methodist Chapel. I went to the service and was invited to take speak. Through the word of the **Lord**, faith was planted in the hearts of all those people, and then something happened. They all knew that young man by name and they all said, "Matthew will be raised up!"

That led me to see that faith could be created in others just as it had been created in me, and I went back to that house and said, "Have you put his clothes to dry?" I think they were a little ashamed that they had done nothing, so they got out his clothes and put them before the **FIRE**.

Then I went into the room and told the young man the vision I had and said that something would happen different from anything that I had experienced before. I said, "When I place my hands on you the glory of the **Lord** will fill the place till I shall not be able to stand. I shall be helpless on the floor." I went out and got his clothes, and said to one of the household, "All I want you to do is, put his stockings on him."

Why I had asked them to put his stockings on is a mystery. His legs were like those of a skeleton and I saw his helplessness, and knew that a miracle would have to be performed. After this member of the household had put the stockings on the young man I said, "Now you can leave the room."

They shut the door. I think it is a very important thing to have the door shut when you have a case like this to deal with, for then you know that you are shut in with only **God** for help. I prayed for the vision the **Lord** had given me to be made good, and instantly, the moment I touched the young man, the power of **God** filled the room and was so powerful that I fell to the floor. My nose and my mouth were touching the floor **and I lay there in the glory unable to move for a quarter of an hour.**

All that while Matthew in the bed was shouting, "**Lord**, this is for thy glory! This is for thy glory!" The bed simply shook, as did everything in the room, by the power of **God**. Matthew's strength, his life, and his heart (which was considered the weakest thing about him) were all renewed. I was still on the floor in the glory when he arose from his bed and began to dress. After he was dressed he began to walk up and down the room shouting, "I'm raised up for thy glory! I'm raised up for thy glory!"

Opening the door he shouted, "Dad, **God** has healed me.

I'm healed!" The same glory filled the kitchen; the **Father** and mother fell down; and the daughter who had been brought from the asylum and whose mind was still affected was made perfectly whole that day.

That whole village was moved, and a revival began that day. I went into that village unnoticed and unknown, but when I left all the village turned out and shouted, "Please come back, please come back, and stop with us longer next time."

I made the nine miles back to Grantham and paid a visit to one of our converts who had moved to this city. The moment I got to the door she said, "My brother is going to take you to a man who has cancer on the bladder." I went with her brother to the house of a sick man and before I reached the house I could hear a voice crying out, "Oh dear! Oh dear! Oh dear!" It was so loud I could hear it at least 50 yards before I got to the home. When I got into his room he was still shouting, "Oh dear! Oh dear!"

Instantly **God** revealed to me that neither this man nor his wife was saved, so I said to the man, "This great affliction is as much mental trouble as cancer. Are you saved?"

"Oh," he cried, "if I were saved, I could die comfortably. If I were saved, I would not mind this cancer or anything."

I shared the way of salvation and **God** saved the man and his wife. That man had such a revelation of salvation that joy overflowed, and I could hear him shouting "Hallelujah" for 50 yards after I left that home. The transformation was beyond all description. He had no more trouble with that cancer. I hurried to the train station and just caught my train back to Bradford.

I soon saw that my plumbing business would have to be second place to the ministry that **God** was giving me. I had supported my family with my plumbing business; but I was called out of town so often, and people could not wait—they had to seek help from other sources. Each time I returned to Bradford I had less business.

There came a period of very severe cold. I went around to my various customers and helped them to cover up their water pipes so they could get water during the cold weather, but I knew that when the thaw came, I should be wanted at many places to repair broken pipes.

I was invited to a convention at Preston in Lancashire. During those convention days the cold broke and telegrams began coming in asking me to return immediately to Bradford to do repair work. At that time the leader of the convention said to me, "You've helped us much and have been a very great blessing, and we would very much like you to stop until the end of the convention; but if you feel you want to go home, we will relieve you."

Smith Wigglesworth When the FIRE Fell

I went home but I found out that most of my customers who had had broken pipes had been compelled to seek other plumbers. There was only one woman, a widow, who had not been able to get a plumber. I went to her house and found that it was flooded with water and that one of the ceilings was down. I was so sorry for her that I repaired her pipes and her roof. She was grateful, for she had waited many days for help. When she said, "Tell me how much I owe you now," I answered, "I won't receive any pay from you. I'll make this an offering to the **Lord** as my last plumbing job."

A friend once remarked: "All the people who say they live by faith seem to have their shoes worn out, and their clothes are old and green." I believed that **God** would abundantly provide if I served him faithfully. I promised him at that time that I would obey him implicitly, but I laid down the condition that my shoe heels must never be a disgrace, and I must never have to wear trousers with the knees out.

I said to the **Lord**, "If either of these things take place, I'll go back to plumbing." He has never failed to supply all my needs. He increased my vision and faith and gave me calls all over England. I was a pioneer with the Pentecostal message to a great many assemblies throughout Great Britain. Soon calls began to pour in from other countries also.

I had a lot of money on my books that I was not able to collect without court action, but I preferred losing it to going to law. All the debts that I owed at that time were met by a young friend whose heart the **Lord** opened to make me a gift of some 50 pounds. My wife and I continued our ministry at Bowland Street, Bradford, even though I had to be frequently absent because I was ministering elsewhere. I believed in house-to-house visitation, and I prayed in every house I entered. Everywhere I went souls were saved and people were healed.

I was not ashamed of the gospel so I purchased the largest flagpole that could be obtained and placed it outside the mission. I had a flag waving on that pole 3 yards long and 1½ yards wide. One side of the flag was red and the other side was blue with white letters. On one side I had the scripture, "I am the **Lord** that healeth thee." [Ex 15.26] On the other side, "Christ died for our sins." [1Co 15.3] That flag had great effect on the people who saw it when passing by.

God moved me on to a place of increasing faith, causing me to see that the word of **God** was written to show us how to act on the principles of faith. I saw that Christ had said,

"When thou makest a feast, call the poor, the maimed, the lame, the blind: and thou shalt be blessed; for they cannot recompense thee: for thou shalt be recompensed at the resurrection of the just." [Lk 14.13-14]

So I engaged two people to go out and find all the needy, the sick, and the afflicted and I gave them tickets inviting them to a banquet and entertainment at the Bowland Street mission.

After the two people had gone round the neighborhood they gathered together a great company of needy people. That sight was beyond all description. **There were the blind and the halt and the withered. [Jn 5.3]** All around the mission there were wheelchairs and people on crutches and the blind were being led. This was the best day in my life up to that point. I wept and wept and wept. One reason I wept was because of the great need; I was weeping also for joy at the opportunity, and with expectation of seeing things that I had never seen before. And so it was.

The first thing we did was to supply everybody with a first-class meal and there was plenty to spare of the very best we could provide. After they were filled, we gave them entertainment, not in a worldly sense, but the whole program was surely very entertaining. The first man on the program was one who had been wheeled up and down in a chair for a very long time, who told how he had been healed by the power of **God**.

 The next one on the program was a woman who had been healed of an issue of blood. She told how she was healed by prayer and by the anointing of oil the day before she was to go on the operating table.

Then we had a man who had been going about trailing his foot and his arm because he had had a paralytic stroke. He told how he was healed after the doctors had given him up.

For an hour and a half, we kept those poor helpless people deeply moved and weeping by the stories they heard of how **Jesus** could heal the sick. I said to them, "Now we have been entertaining you today, but we are going to have another meeting next Saturday and you people who are today bound and who have come in wheelchairs, and some of you folks who have come like the woman in the gospel who had spent all she had on doctors and was no better, are going to entertain us on Saturday night by the stories of the freedom that you have received today by the name of **Jesus** Christ." So we prayed for those people and **God** mightily met us. We surely had a great time the following Saturday night as one after another told of how **God** had healed them of their different infirmities.

I shall never forget that day. I cried out, "Who wants to be healed?" Of course, everyone wanted to be. I remember one case. I had gone to fetch a woman in her wheelchair. The wheel was broken, but I managed to fix it up. I helped her from her home, but that wheelchair gave way in the road. I said to her, "Well, you will never want it again anyhow." I fixed it again and ultimately, we arrived at the mission. **God** so marvelously healed her that she walked home, and I am a witness to the fact that she went up all the steps into her house and into her bedroom, praising the **Lord** as she went.

There was one young man who had been having epileptic fits for eighteen years, who was instantly healed. He had never gone out without having someone to accompany him. His mother brought him to that meeting, and **God** so wonderfully undertook for him that within two weeks he was working in a factory and bringing home wages.

Another case was that of a young man who was all doubled up like the woman in the Bible. The **Lord Jesus** called it the spirit of infirmity, [Lk 13.11] indicating that she was bound by an evil spirit. That day that young man was loosed and set free just as the woman was loosed in the synagogue. Christ in his healing ministry said he was working the works of **God**, and he said that if we believed, we also could do the works of **God**. [Jn 14.12] He had cast out the spirit of infirmity; so I cast out the spirit of infirmity in the name of **Jesus** Christ, and immediately the young man was made straight, and everyone was blessing the **Lord** for the miracle they saw.

Another remarkable case was that of a boy who, from his head to his feet, was encased in thin iron. The building was very crowded, but the **Father** lifted up the boy in the iron case and passed him over to the man who was sitting in the seat in front of him. He was then passed on to the next seat and others passed him on until ultimately, he was placed before me on the platform. I anointed him with oil and laid hands on him in the name of the **Lord Jesus**, and immediately he cried out, "Papa, Papa, Papa. It's going all over me! It's going all over me! It's going all over me!" And he was loosened that day and made absolutely free.

Can you wonder that faith was quickened in the hearts of many as they saw these miracles wrought? A week after, these people were going around as witnesses telling what Christ had done for them.

The Way of faith

In Romans 4:16 we read, "It is of faith, that it might be by grace," meaning that we can open the door and **God** will come in. What will happen if we open the door by faith? **God** is greater than our thoughts. He puts it to us, "Exceeding abundantly above all that we ask or think." When we ask a lot, **God** says "more."

 Are we ready for the "more"? And then the "much more"? We may be, or we may miss it. We may be so endued by the Spirit of the **Lord** in the morning that it shall be a tonic for the whole day. **God** can so thrill us with new life that nothing ordinary or small will satisfy us after that. There is a great place for us in **God** where we won't be satisfied with small things.

We won't have any satisfaction unless the **FIRE** falls, and whenever we pray we will have the assurance that what we have prayed for is going to follow the moment we open our mouth. Oh this praying in the Spirit! This great plan of **God** for us! In a moment we can go right in. In where? Into His will. Then all things will be well.

You can't get anything asleep these days. The world is always awake, and we should always be awake to what **God** has for us. Awake to take! Awake to hold it after we get it! How much can you take? We know that **God** is more willing to give than we are to receive. How shall we dare to be asleep when the Spirit commands us to take everything on the table. It is the greatest banquet that ever was and ever will be—the table where all you take only leaves more behind. A fullness that cannot be exhausted! How many are prepared for a lot?

"And **Jesus** entered into Jerusalem, and into the temple: and when he had looked round about upon all things, and now the eventide was come, he went out unto Bethany with the twelve. And on the morrow, when they were come from Bethany, he was hungry: and seeing a fig tree afar off having leaves, he came, if haply he might find anything thereon: and when he came to it, he found nothing but leaves; for the time of figs was not yet. And **Jesus** answered and said, No man eat fruit of thee hereafter forever. And his disciples heard it." Mark 11:11-14.

Jesus was sent from **God** to meet the world's need. **Jesus** lived to minister life by the words He spoke. He said to Philip, "He that hath seen me hath seen the **Father**… the words that I speak unto you, I speak not of myself: but the **Father** that dwelleth in me." I am persuaded that if we are filled with His words of life and the **Holy Ghost**, and Christ is made manifest in our mortal flesh, then the **Holy Ghost** can move us with His life, His words, till as He was, so are we in the world. We are receiving our life from **God**, and it is always kept in tremendous activity, working in our whole nature as we live in perfect contact with **God**.

Jesus spoke, and everything He said must come to pass.

That is a great plan. When we are filled only with the **Holy Spirit**, and we won't allow the Word of **God** to be detracted by what we hear or by what we read, then comes the inspiration, then the life, then the activity, then the glory! Oh to live in it! To live in it is to be moved by it. To live in it is to be moved so that we will have **God's** life, **God's** personality in the human body.

By the grace of **God** I want to impart the Word, and bring you into a place where you will dare to act upon the plan of the Word, to so breathe life by the power of the Word that it is impossible for you to go on under any circumstances without His provision. The most difficult things that come to us are to our advantage from **God's** side.

When we come to the place of impossibilities, it is the grandest place for us to see the possibilities of **God**. Put this right in your mind and never forget it. You will never be of any importance to **God** till you venture in the impossible. **God** wants people on the daring line. I do not mean foolish daring. "Be filled with the Spirit," and when we are filled with the Spirit, we are not so much concerned about the secondary thing. It is the first with **God**.

Everything of evil, everything unclean, everything Satanic in any way is an objectionable thing to **God**, and we are to live above it, destroy it, not to allow it to have any place. **Jesus** didn't let the devil answer back. We must reach the place where we will not allow anything to interfere with the plan of **God**.

Smith Wigglesworth When the FIRE Fell

Jesus and His disciples came to the tree. It looked beautiful. It had the appearance of the fruit, but when He came to it, He found nothing but leaves. He was very disappointed. Looking at the tree, He spoke to it: Here is shown forth His destructive power.

"No man eat the fruit of thee hereafter forever." The next day they were passing by the same way, and the disciples saw the tree "dried up from the roots." They said to **Jesus**, "Behold, the fig tree which thou cursedst is withered away." And **Jesus** said, "Have faith in **God**."

There isn't a person that has ever seen a tree dried from the root. Trees always show the first signs of death right at the top. But the Master had spoken. The Master dealt with a natural thing to reveal to these disciples a supernatural plan. If He spoke, it would have to obey. And, **God**, the **Holy Ghost**, wants us to understand clearly that we are the mouthpiece of **God** and are here for His divine plan.

We may allow the natural mind to dethrone that, but in the measure we do, we won't come into the treasure which **God** has for us. The Word of **God** must have first place. It must not have a second place. In any measure that we doubt the Word of **God**, from that moment we have ceased to thrive spiritually and actively. The Word of **God** is not only to be looked at and read but received as the Word of **God** to become life right within our life. "Thy word have I hid in my heart that I might not sin against thee."

"I give unto you power… over all the power of the

enemy." Luke 10:19. There it is. We can accept or reject it. I accept and believe it. It is a word beyond all human calculation: "Have faith in **God**." These disciples were in the Master's school.

They were the men who were to turn the world upside down. As we receive the Word we will never be the same; if we dare to act as the Word goes forth and not be afraid, then **God** will honor us. "The **Lord** of hosts is with us; the **God** of Jacob is our refuge." Jacob was the weakest of all, in any way you like to take it. He is the **God** of Jacob, and He is our **God**. So we may likewise have our names changed to Israel.

As the **Lord Jesus** injected this wonderful word, "Have faith in **God**," into the disciples, He began to show how it was to be. Looking around about Him He saw the mountains, and He began to bring a practical application. Truth means nothing unless it moves us. We can have our minds filled a thousand times, but it must get into our hearts if there are to be any results. All inspiration is in the heart. All compassion is in the heart.

Looking at the mountains, He said, "Shall not doubt in his heart." That is the barometer. You know exactly where you are. The man knows when he prays. If his heart is right how it leaps. No man is any good for **God** and never makes progress in **God** who does not hate sin. You are never safe. But there is a place in **God** where you can love righteousness and where you can hate iniquity till the Word of **God** is a light in your bosom, quickening every fiber of your body, thrilling your whole nature. The pure in heart see **God**. Believe in the heart!

What a word! If I believe in my heart **God** says I can begin to speak, and "whatsoever" I say shall come to pass.

Here is an act of believing in the heart. I was called to Halifax, England, to pray for a lady missionary. I found it an urgent call. I could see faith was absent, and I could see there was death: Death is a terrible thing, and **God** wants to keep us alive. I know it is appointed unto man once to die, but I believe in a rapturous death. I said to the woman, "How are you?" She said, "I have faith," in a very weak tone of voice. "Faith? Why are you dying? Brother Walshaw, is she dying?" "Yes." "Nurse, is she dying?" "Yes." To a friend standing by, "Is she dying?" "Yes."

Now I believe there is something in a heart that is against defeat, and this is the faith which **God** hath given to us. I said to her, "In the name of **Jesus**, now believe and you'll live." She said, "I believe," and **God** sent life from her head to her feet. They dressed her, and she lived.

"Have faith." It isn't saying you have faith. It is he that believeth in his heart. It is a grasping of the eternal **God**. Faith is **God** in the human vessel. "This is the victory that overcometh the world, even our faith." 1 John 5:4. He that believeth overcomes the world. "Faith cometh by hearing, and hearing by the Word of **God**." He that believeth in his heart!

Can you imagine anything easier than that? He that believeth in his heart! What is the process? Death! No one can live who believes in his heart. He dies to everything worldly. He that loves the world is not of **God**. You can measure the whole thing up, and examine yourself to see if you have faith. Faith is life. Faith enables you to lay hold of that which is and get it out of the way for **God** to bring in something that is not.

Just before I left home, I was in Norway. A woman wrote to me from England saying she had been operated on for cancer three years before, but that it was now coming back. She was living in constant dread of the whole thing as the operation was so painful. Would it be possible to see me when I returned to England? I wrote that I would be passing through London on the 20th of June last year.

If she would like to meet me at the hotel, I would pray for her. She replied that she would be going to London to be there to meet me. When I met this woman, I saw she was in great pain, and I have great sympathy for people who have tried to get relief and have failed. If you preachers lose your compassion you can stop preaching, for it won't be any good.

You will only be successful as a preacher as you let your heart become filled with the compassion of **Jesus**. As soon as I saw her, I entered into the state of her mind. I saw how distressed she was. She came to me in a mournful spirit, and her whole face was downcast. I said to her, "There are two things going to happen today. One is that you are to know that you are sayed." "Oh, if I could only know I was saved," she said. "There is another thing. You have to go out of this hotel without pain, without a trace of cancer."

Then I began with the Word. Oh, this wonderful Word! We do not have to go up to bring Him down; neither do we have to go down to bring Him up. "The word is nigh thee, even in thy mouth, and in thy heart: that is, the word of faith, which we preach." Romans 10:8. I said, "Believe that He took your sins when He died at the cross.

Believe that when He was buried, it was for you. Believe that when He arose, it was for you. And now at **God's** right hand, He is sitting for you. If you can believe in your heart and confess with your mouth, you shall be saved." She looked at me saying, "Oh, it is going all through my body. I know I am saved now. If He comes today, I'll go how I have dreaded, the thought of His coming all my life! But if He comes today, I know I shall be ready."

The first thing was finished. Now for the second. I laid my hands upon her in the name of **Jesus**, believing in my heart that I could say what I wanted and it should be done. I said, "In the name of **Jesus**, I cast this out." She jumped up. "Two things have happened," she said. "I am saved, and now the cancer is gone."

What works in us through being one with him, rooted and grounded? Perfect love, and perfect love has justice wrapped up in it, and the day is coming when the saints will say "Amen" to the judgments of God.

CHAPTER THREE

**Faith will stand amid the wrecks of time,
Faith unto eternal glories climb;
Only count the promise true,
And the Lord will stand by you—
Faith will win the victory every time!**

So many people have nervous trouble. I'll tell you how to get rid of your nervous trouble. I have something in my bag, one dose of which will cure you. "I am the **Lord** that healeth thee." How this wonderful Word of **God** changes the situation. "Perfect love casteth out fear." "There is no fear in love."

I have tested that so often, casting out the whole condition of fear and the whole situation has been changed. We have a big **God**; only He has to be absolutely and only trusted. The people who do believe **God** are strong, and "he that hath clean hands shall be stronger and stronger."

At the close of a certain meeting, a man said to me, "You have helped everybody but me. I wish you would help me." "What's the trouble with you?" "I cannot sleep because of nervous trouble. My wife says she has not known me to have a full night's sleep for three years. I am just shattered." Anybody could tell he was.

I put my hands upon him and said, "Brother I believe in my heart. Go home and sleep in the name of **Jesus**." "I can't sleep." "Go home and sleep in the name of **Jesus**." "I can't sleep." The lights were being put out, and I took the man by the coat collar and said, "Don't talk to me any more." That was sufficient. He went after that. When he got home his mother and wife said to him, "What has happened?" "Nothing. He helped everybody but me." "Surely he said something to you." "He told me to come home and sleep in the name of **Jesus**, but you know I can't sleep in anything."

His wife urged him to do what I had said, and he had scarcely got his head on the pillow before the **Lord** put him to sleep. The next morning he was still asleep. The next morning he was still asleep. She began to make a noise in the bedroom to awaken him, but he did not waken. Sunday morning he was still asleep. She did what every good wife would do. She decided to make a good Sunday dinner and then awaken him. After the dinner was prepared, she went up to him and put her hand on his shoulder and shook him, saying, "Are you never going to wake up?" From that night that man never had any more nervousness.

A man came to me for whom I prayed. Then I asked, "Are you sure you are perfectly healed?" "Well," he said, "there is just a little pain in my shoulder." "Do you know what that is?" I asked him. "That is unbelief. Were you saved before you believed or after?" "After." "You will be healed after." "It is all right now," he said, It was all right before, but he hadn't believed.

The Word of **God** is for us. It is by faith that it might be by grace.

YOUNG MAN ON FIRE

There was a young man at the meeting this night who had been saved the night before. He was all on **FIRE** to get others saved and purposed in his heart that every day of his life he would get someone saved. He saw this dejected hangman and began to speak to him about his soul. He brought him down to our mission and there he came under a wonderful and mighty conviction of sin. For two and a half hours he was literally sweating under conviction and you could see a vapor rising up from him in the cold air. At the end of two and a half hours he was graciously saved.

I said, "**Lord**, tell me what to do now." The **Lord** said, "Don't leave him, but go home with him." I went to his house. When he saw his wife he said, "**God** has saved me." The wife broke down and she too was graciously saved. I tell you there was a difference in that home.

Even the cat knew the difference.

There were two sons in that house and one of them said to his mother, "Mother, what is happening here in our home? It has never like then this before. It is so peaceful. What is it?" She told him, "**Father** has been gloriously saved." Both sons were gloriously saved.

I took this man with me to many special services and the power of **God** was on him for many days. He would give his testimony and as he grew in grace he desired to preach the gospel. He became a powerful evangelist and hundreds and hundreds were brought to a saving knowledge of the **Lord Jesus** Christ through his ministry.

The grace of **God** is sufficient for the vilest. He can take the most wicked of men and make them monuments of his grace. He did this with Saul of Tarsus at the very time he was breathing out threatening's and slaughter against the disciples of the **Lord**. He did it with Berry the hangman. He will do it for hundreds more in response to our cries.

A FLAME OF FIRE

I was traveling from Egypt to Italy. **God** was visiting me wonderfully on this ship, and every hour I was conscious of His blessed presence. A man on the ship collapsed and his wife was terribly alarmed, and everybody else was panicking. Some said that he was about to expire. But I saw it was just a glorious opportunity for the power of

God to be manifested. Oh, what it means to be a flame of **FIRE**, to be indwelt by the living Christ!

We are in a bad condition if we have to pray for power when an occasion like this comes along, or if we have to wait until we feel a sense of His presence. The **Lord**'s promise was, **"Ye shall receive power after that the Holy Ghost is come upon you,"** and if we will believe, the power of **God** will be always manifested when there is a definite need. When you exercise your faith, you will find that there is the greater power in you than that is in the world. Oh, to be awakened out of unbelief into a place of daring for **God** on the authority of His blessed Book and the redemptive work of Christ!

So right there on board that ship, in the name of **Jesus** I rebuked the devil, and to the astonishment of the man's wife and the man himself, he was able to stand. He said, "What is this? It is going all over me. I have never felt anything like this before." From the top of his head to the soles of his feet the power of **God** shook him. **God** has given us authority over all the power of the devil. Oh, that we may live in the place where we realize this always, and that were completely submitted to that authority!

FLAMES OF FIRE

Some years ago I was in Ceylon. In one place the folk complained, "Four days is not enough to be with us."

"No," I said, "but it is a better than nothing." They said to me, "We are not touching the multitudes of people who are here." I said, "Can you have a meeting early in the morning, at eight o'clock?" They said they could and would if I so desired. So I said, "Tell all the mothers who want their babies to be healed to come, and all the people over seventy to come, and after that we hope to give an address to the people to make them ready for the Baptism in the Spirit."

It would have done you good to see the four hundred mothers coming at eight o'clock in the morning with their babies, and then to see the hundred and fifty old people, with their white hair, coming to be healed. We need to have something more than smoke and huff and puff to touch the people; we need to be a burning **FIRE** for **God**. His ministers must be **FLAMES** of **FIRE**. In those days there were thousands out to hear the Word of **God**. I believe there were about three thousand persons crying for mercy at once that day. It was a great sight.

From that first morning on the meetings grew to such an extent that I would estimate every time some 5,000 to 6,000 gathered; and I had to preach in a temperatures of 110 degrees. Then I had to pray for these people who were sick. But I can tell you, a flame of **FIRE** can do anything. Things change in the **FIRE**. This was Pentecost.

But what moved me more than anything else was this: there were hundreds who tried to touch me, they were so impressed with the power of **God** that was present. And many testified that with the touch they were healed, It was not that there was any virtue in me—the people's faith was exercised as it was at Jerusalem when they said Peter's shadow would heal them.

Smith - "Repeat in your heart often: "baptized with the Holy Ghost and FIRE, FIRE, FIRE!" All the unction, and weeping, and travailing comes through the baptism of FIRE, and I say to you and say to myself, purged and cleansed and filled with renewed spiritual power." "Who makes his ministers a flame of FIRE." Heb. 1:7

The place of power

God is looking, **God** is wanting men and women who are willing to submit, and SUBMIT, and SUBMIT, and yield, and YIELD, and YIELD to the **Holy Spirit** until their bodies are saturated and soaked through and through with **God**, until you realize that **God** your **Father** has you in such condition that at any moment He can reveal His will to you and communicate whatever He wants to say to you.

God wants us to be in a place where the least breath of heaven makes us all on **FIRE**, ready for everything. You say, "How can I have that?" Oh, you can have that as easy as anything. "Can I?" Yes, it is as simple as possible. "How?" Let heaven come in.

Let the **Holy Ghost** take possession of you, and

when He comes into your body you will find out that that is the keynote of the spirit of joy and the spirit of rapture, and if you will allow the **Holy Ghost** to have full control you will find you are living in the Spirit.

You will find out that the opportunities will be **God's** opportunities, and there is a difference between **God's** opportunities and ours. You will find you have come to the right place at the right time, and you will speak the right word at the right time and in the right place, and you will not go a warfare at your own charge.

A FIRE BROKE OUT

A preacher, suffering many days from the kick of a horse, walking with great pain and in much distress, made a special call at the hotel in which I was staying, and being led by the Spirit, according to **God's** Word, I laid hands on the bruised ankle. A **FIRE** broke out with burning and healing power, and from that moment on he could walk easily and without pain.

"If you want to increase in the life of God, then you must settle it in your heart that you will not at any time resist the Holy Spirit. The Holy Ghost and FIRE - the FIRE burning up everything that would impoverish and destroy you."

GOD COMES WITH FIRE

We should carefully consider what the apostle said to us, "Grieve not the **Holy Spirit**, whereby ye are sealed unto the day of redemption." The sealing of the **Holy Spirit** is very remarkable and I pray **God** that not one person may lose the divine inheritance that **God** has chosen for you. There is nothing greater than this. **God's** mind is vastly greater than yours. His thoughts are higher than the heavens over you, so that you need not be afraid.

Isaiah 55:9 For as the heavens are higher than the earth, so are my ways higher than your ways, and my thoughts than your thoughts.

I have a great love for my boys, and great love for my daughter; but it is nothing in comparison to **God's** love toward us. **God's** love is desirous that we should walk up and down in the earth as His Son **Jesus** did, clothed, filled, radiant, with **FIRE** beaming forth from our countenance, manifesting the power of the Spirit, so that the people will experience complete liberty.

But there is deplorable ignorance today among those who have the **Holy Ghost**. It is not right for you to think that because you have a gift from the **Holy Ghost** that you are to wave it before the people, and try to get their minds upon that, because if you do you will be out of the will of **God**. Gifts and callings may be given to us without repentance but remember that **God** calls you to give an account for the gifts being properly administered in a spiritual way after you have received it.

It is not given to adorn you, but to sustain you, to build, to edify and to bless the church. When the church receives this edification and **God** ministers through that member, then all the members will rejoice together. **God** moves upon us as His offspring, as His choice, and fruit of the earth. He wants us to be decked in wonderful raiment, even as our Master **Jesus**.

Gods operations upon us may be painful but the wise saint will remember that among those whom **God** chastens, it is the one who is exercised by that chastening to whom "it yieldeth the peaceable fruit of righteousness." Therefore let Him do with you what seems good to Him, for He has His hand upon you and He will not willingly take it off till He has performed the thing He knows you need.

So if He comes with **FIRE**, be ready for the **FIRE**. If He comes with chastisement, be ready for chastisement. If He comes with correction, be ready for correction. Whatever He wills to do, let Him do it and He will bring you to the land of plenty. Oh, it is worth the world to be under the power and influence of the **Holy Ghost**!

If **God** chastens you not, if you sail smoothly along without incident, without crosses, without persecutions, without trials, remember that "if ye be without chastisement, whereof all are partakers, then are ye bastards and not sons." Hebrews 12:8. Therefore "Examine yourselves whether ye be in the faith." Never forget that **Jesus** said this word: "They that hear My voice, follow Me." **Jesus** wants all of us to follow him.

He wants us to have the evidence of His presence in our testimony.

We are called to be eternally saved by the power of **God**. Do not be led astray by anything, do not go by your feelings for your salvation, and do not take anybody's word for your salvation. Believe that **God's** Word is true. What does it say?

"He that hath the Son hath life; he that hath not the Son shall not see life, but the wrath of God abideth upon him."

When your will becomes entirely swallowed up in the will of **God**, then you are clearly in the place where the **Holy Ghost** can make **Jesus Lord** in your life, **Lord** over your purchases, **Lord** over your selling, **Lord** over your eating and your drinking, your clothing and your choice of companionship.

THE CHURCH MUST BE FULL OF FIRE

Any church who hinders the working of the Spirit in their services will surely cause the work of **God** to dry up. The church must be as free in the Spirit as possible. We must allow a certain amount of extravagance when people are getting ahold of **God**. Unless we are very wise, we can easily interfere and quench the power of **God** which is upon us. It is an evident fact that when one man in a meeting, filled with unbelief, will make a place for the devil to interfere.

If you want a church full of life you must have one in which the Spirit of **God** is manifested. And in order to keep **FIRE** ignited from that blessed incarnation of the Spirit, you must be as simple as babies; you must be as harmless as doves and as wise as serpents (Matthew 10:16).

I always ask **God** for a leading of His grace. It takes grace to be in a meeting because it is so easy if you are not careful, to get into the natural thinking realm. A man who is a preacher, if he has lost the unction of the Spirit, will be restored if he will repent and get right with **God**, and get the unction back.

It never pays us to be less than always spiritual, and we must have a divine language and the language must be of **God**. Beloved, if you come into the will of **God**, with the grace of **God**, one thing will certainly take place in your life. You will change from that old attitude of the world's philosophy where you were judging everybody, and where you were abrasive with everyone. And come into a place where you will have a heart that under no circumstances reviles again when you are reviled.

I know Godly people who think before they speak or respond. Here is a great word: **"For your obedience is come abroad unto all men. I am glad therefore on your behalf: but yet I would have you wise unto that which is good, and simple concerning evil" (Romans 16:19).**

You have come to the place where there is No inward corruption or defilement, that is full of distrusts. But you have attained a holy, divine likeness of **Jesus** that dares believe that **God** Almighty will surely watch over all. Hallelujah!

"There shall no evil befall thee, neither shall any plague come nigh thy dwelling. For He shall give his angels charge over thee, to keep thee in all thy ways" (Psalm 91:10,11).

The child of **God** who is founded in the bosom of the **Father** has the sweetest touch of heaven, and the honey of the Word is always manifested in him.

If the saints only knew how precious they are in the sight of **God** they would scarcely be able to sleep for thinking of His watchful, loving care. Oh, He **Jesus** is so precious! He is our wonderful and lovely Savior! He is divine in all of His attitude toward us and makes our hearts to burn. There is nothing like it. "Oh," they said on the road to Emmaus, "did not our heart burn within us, as He walked with us and talked with us?" (Luke 24:32). Oh beloved, it must be so today.

Always keep in your mind the fact that the **Holy Ghost** wants to bring forth manifestations. We must understand that the **Holy Ghost** is the breath of **God**, the **Holy Ghost** is a Person, and it is the most marvelous thing to me to know that this **Holy Ghost** power can be in every part of your body. You can feel it from the crown of your head to the soles of your feet. Oh, it is lovely to be filled with the **FIRE** of the **Holy Ghost**! And when that takes place out tongue must give forth the glory and the praise **God** deserves.

Smith Wigglesworth When the FIRE Fell

We must come into the place of magnifying the **Lord**. The **Holy Ghost** is the great Magnifier, and exalter of all that is of **Jesus**. He is the great Illuminator of **Jesus**. And so after the **Holy Ghost** comes in, it is impossible to keep your tongue quiet. Why, you would explode if you did not give utterance to your joy.

Talk about a dumb baptized soul? Such a person is not to be found in the Scriptures. You will find that when you speak unto **God** in the new tongue He gives you, you enter into a close communion with Him hitherto never experienced. Talk about preaching!

I would like to know how it will be possible for all the people filled with the **Holy Ghost** to stop preaching. Even the sons and daughters must prophesy. After the **Holy Ghost** comes in, a man is in a new world with **God**. And you will find it so real that you will want to sing, talk, laugh, and shout. We are in a supernatural place when the **Holy Ghost** comes in.

If the incoming of the Spirit is lovely, what must be the overflow? The incoming is meant to be an overflow. I am very interested in scenery. When I was in Switzerland I wouldn't be satisfied till I went to the top of the mountain, though I like the valleys also. On the summit of the mountain the sun beats on the snow and sends the water trickling down the mountains right through to the meadows. Go there and see if you can stop it. It is Just so in the spiritual. **God** begins with the divine flow of His eternal power which is the **Holy Ghost**, and you cannot stop it.

We must with our whole heart believe that the baptism of the Holy Ghost is meant to make us FLAMES of FIRE.

Peter and John had been baptized only a short time. Did they truly know what they had? No, and I defy you to know what you have. No one knows what he has in the baptism of the **Holy Ghost**. You have no conception of it. You cannot measure it by any human standards. It is greater than any man has any idea of. Peter and John had no idea what they had. For the first time after they were baptized in the **Holy Ghost** they came down to the Gate Beautiful.

There they saw the man sitting who for forty years had been lame from his mother's womb. What was the first thing they knew after they saw him? He needed a Miracle. What was the second? **God** was more than able. What was the third? Deal with it by Faith in and by the Authority of **Jesus** Christ in the power of the **Holy Ghost**. There is no other way. You will always find this three-step order in the Scripture for every situation.

We desperately need spiritual giants in the earth, mighty in apprehension, amazing in activity, and always having a wonderful report because of their faith in Christ. But I find instead that there are many people who perhaps have some discernment, some knowledge of the Word, but they have failed to put it into practice, so these gifts lie dormant.

 I am here to help you to begin to apprehend this divine

life with mighty acts by the power of **God** through the gifts of the **Holy Spirit**. You will find that what I am speaking on is out of my personal experiences that I have derived from wonderful meetings in many lands. The man who is filled with the **Holy Ghost** is always acting. You read the first verse of the Acts of the Apostles, "**Jesus** began both to do and teach." He began to do first, and so must we.

Bible evidence of the Baptism of the Spirit

There is much controversy today as regards to the genuineness of the Pentecostal work, but there is nothing so convincing as the fact that over fifteen years ago a revival of the **Holy Ghost** began and has never ceased. You will find that in every place throughout the world **God** has poured out His **Spirit** in a remarkable way in a way parallel with the glorious revival that started the church of the first century.

People, who could not understand what **God** was doing when He kept them gathered in prayer, wondered as these days were being brought about by the **Holy Ghost**, and found themselves in exactly the same place and entering into an identical experience as the Apostles on the day of Pentecost.

Our **Lord Jesus** said to His disciples, "Behold, I send the promise of My **Father** upon you: but tarry ye in the city of Jerusalem, until ye be endued with power from on high" (Luke 24:49). **God** promised through the prophet Joel, "I will pour out My **Spirit** upon all flesh... Upon the servants and upon the handmaids in those days will I pour out My **Spirit**." As there is a widespread misconception concerning this receiving of the **Holy Spirit**, I believe the **Lord** would have us examine the Scriptures on this subject.

You know, beloved, it had to be something based on solid facts to move me. I was as certain as possible that I had received the **Holy Ghost** and was absolutely rigid in this conviction. When this Pentecostal outpouring began in England I went to Sunderland and met with the people who had assembled for the purpose of receiving the **Holy Ghost**. I was continually in those meetings causing disturbances until the people wished I had never come.

They said that I was disturbing the meetings. But I was hungry and thirsty for **God**, and had gone to Sunderland because I heard that **God** was pouring out His **Spirit** in a new way. I heard that **God** had now visited His people, had manifested His power and that people were speaking in tongues as on the day of Pentecost.

When I got to this place I said, "I cannot understand this meeting. I have left a meeting in Bradford all on **FIRE** for **God**. The **FIRE** fell last night and we were all laid out under the power of **God**. I have come here for tongues, and I don't hear them-I don't hear anything."

"Oh!" they said, "when you get baptized with the **Holy Ghost** you will speak in tongues." "Oh, is that it?" said I, "when the presence of **God** came upon me, my tongue was loosened, and really I felt as I went in the open air to preach that I had a new tongue." "Ah no," they said, "That is not it." "What is it, then?" I asked. They said, "When you get baptized in the **Holy Ghost-**" "I am baptized," I interjected, "and there is no one here who can persuade me that I am not baptized." So I was up against them and they were up against me.

I remember a man getting up and saying, "You know, brothers and sisters, I was here three weeks and then the **Lord** baptized me with the **Holy Ghost** and I began to speak with other tongues." I said, "Let us hear it. That's what I'm here for." But he would not talk in tongues. I was doing what others are doing today, confusing the 12th of I Corinthians with the 2nd of Acts.

These two chapters deal with different things, one with the gifts of the **Spirit**, and the other with the Baptism of the **Spirit** with the accompanying sign. I did not understand this and so I said to the man, "Let's hear you speak in tongues." But he could not. He had not received the "gift" of tongues, but the Baptism. (It takes faith to let **God** take control of your tongue)

As the days passed, I became more and more hungry. I had opposed the meetings so much, but the **Lord** was gracious, and I shall ever remember that last day-the day I was to leave. **God** was with me so much that last night. They were to have a meeting and I went, but I could not rest. I went to the Parsonage, and there in the library I said to Mrs. Boddy, "I cannot rest any longer, I must have these tongues." She replied, "Brother Wigglesworth, it is not the tongues you need but the Baptism.

If you will allow **God** to baptize you, the other will

be all right." "My dear sister, I know I am baptized," I said. "You know that I have to leave here at 4 o'clock. Please lay hands on me that I may receive the tongues."

She rose and laid her hands on me and the **FIRE** fell. I said, "The **FIRE'S** falling." Then came a persistent knock at the door, and she had to leave the room. That was the best thing that could have happened, for I was ALONE WITH **GOD**. Then He gave me a revelation.

Oh, it was wonderful! He showed me an empty cross and **Jesus** glorified. I do thank **God** that the cross is empty, that **Christ** is no more on the cross. It was there that He bore the curse, for it is written, "Cursed is everyone that hangeth on a tree."

He became sin for us that we might be made the righteousness of **God** in Him, and now, there He is in the glory. Then I saw that **God** had purified me. It seemed that **God** gave me a new **VISION**, and I saw a perfect being within me with mouth open, saying, "Clean 1 Clean! Clean!" When I began to repeat it I found myself speaking in other tongues. The joy was so great that when I came to utter it my tongue failed, and I began to worship **God** in other tongues as the **Spirit** gave me utterance.

It was all as beautiful and peaceful as when **Jesus** said, "Peace, be still!" and the tranquility of that moment and the joy surpassed anything I had ever known up to that moment. But Hallelujah 1 have in these days I have grown with greater, mightier, more wonderful divine manifestations and power.

That was but the beginning. There is no end to this kind of beginning. You will never get an end to the **Holy Ghost** till you leave this world into glory-till you are right in the presence of **God** forever. And even then, we shall ever be conscious of His presence.

What had I received? I had received the Bible evidence. This Bible evidence is wonderful to me. I knew I had received the very evidence of the **Spirit**'s incoming that the Apostles received on the day of Pentecost. I knew that everything I had up to that time was in the nature of an anointing bringing me in line with **God** in preparation, but now I knew I had the Biblical Baptism in the **Spirit**. It had the backing of the Scriptures. You are always right when you have the backing of the Scriptures and you are never right if you have not a foundation for your testimony in the Word of **God**.

For many years I have thrown out a challenge to any person who can prove to me that he has the Baptism without speaking in tongues as the **Spirit** gives utterance. It must be proved by the Word of **God** that he has been baptized in the **Holy Ghost** without the Bible evidence, but so far no one has accepted the challenge.

I only say this because as many were as I was; they have a rigid idea that they have received the Baptism without the Bible evidence. The **Lord Jesus** wants those who preach the Word to have living the Word. Don't be misled by anything else. Have a Bible proof for all you have, and then you will be in a place where no man can deceive you.

I was so full of joy that I wired home to say that I had

received the **Holy Ghost**. As soon as I got home, my boy came running up to me and said, "**Father**, have you received the **Holy Ghost**?" I said, "Yes, my boy." He said, "Let's hear you speak in tongues." But I could not. Why? I had received the Baptism in the **Spirit** with the speaking in tongues as the Bible evidence according to Acts 2:4, and had not received the gift of Tongues according to 1 Corinthians 12.

I had received the Giver of all gifts. At some time later when I was helping some souls to seek and receive the Baptism of the **Spirit**, **God** gave me the gift of Tongues so that I could speak at any time. I could speak, but will not - no never! I must allow the **Holy Ghost** to use the gift. It should be so, so that we shall have divine utterances only by the **Spirit**. I would be very sorry to use a gift, but the Giver has all power to use the whole nine gifts.

I want to take you to the Scriptures to prove my position. There are business men here, and they know that in cases of law, where there are two clear witnesses they could win a case before any judge in Australia. On the clear evidence of two witnesses any judge will give a verdict. What has **God** given us? Three clear witnesses on the Baptism in the **Holy Spirit**-more than are necessary in law courts.

The first is in Acts 2:4, "They were all filled with tile **Holy Ghost**, and began to speak with other tongues, as the **Spirit** gave them utterance." Here we have the original pattern. And **God** gave to Peter an eternal word that couples this experience with the promise that went before. "This is that." And **God** wants you to have that nothing less than that. He wants you to receive the Baptism in the **Holy Spirit** according to this original Pentecostal pattern.

In Acts 10 we have another witness. Peter is in the house of Cornelius. Cornelius had had a **VISION** of a **Holy** angel and had sent for Peter. A person said to me one day, "You don't admit that I am filled and baptized with the **Holy Ghost**. Why, I was ten days and ten nights on my back before the **Lord** and He was flooding my soul with joy." I said, "Praise the **Lord**, sister, that was only the beginning.

The disciples were tarrying that time, and they were still, and the mighty power of **God** fell upon them then and the Bible tells what happened when the power fell. And that is just what happened in the house of Cornelius. The **Holy Ghost** fell on all them which heard the word. "And they of the circumcision which believed were astonished, as many as came with Peter, because that on the Gentiles was poured out the gift of the **Holy Ghost**."

What convinced these prejudiced Jews that the **Holy Ghost** had come? "For they heard them speak with tongues and magnify **God**." There was no other way for them to know. This evidence could not be contradicted. It is the Bible evidence.

We have heard two witnesses, and that is sufficient to satisfy the world. But **God** goes one better. Let us look at Acts 19:6, "And when Paul had laid his hands upon them, the **Holy Ghost** came on them; and they spake with tongues and prophesied." These Ephesians received the identical Bible evidence as the Apostles at the beginning and they prophesied in addition. Three times the Scriptures show us this evidence of the Baptism in the **Spirit**. I do not magnify tongues. No, by **God's** grace, I magnify the Giver of tongues. And I magnify above all Him whom the **Holy Ghost** has come to reveal to us, the **Lord Jesus Christ**. He it is who sends the **Holy Spirit** and I magnify Him because He makes no difference between us and those at the beginning.

But what are tongues for? Look at the 2nd verse of 1 Cor. 14 and you will see a very blessed truth. Oh, Hallelujah! Have you been there, beloved? I tell you, **God** wants to take you there. "He that speaketh in an unknown tongue, speaketh not unto men, but unto **God**: for no man understandeth him; howbeit in the **Spirit** he speaketh mysteries." It goes on to say, "He that speaketh in an unknown tongue edifieth himself."

Enter the promises of **God**. It is your inheritance. You will do more in one year if you are really filled with the **Holy Ghost** than you could do in fifty years apart from Him.

CHAPTER FOUR

A flame for God

Christ said to His disciples just before He ascended, "Ye shall receive power, after that the **Holy Ghost** is come upon you: and ye shall be witnesses unto Me." On the day of Pentecost He sent the power, and the rest of the Book of the Acts of the Apostles tells of the witnessing of these Spirit-filled disciples, the **Lord** working with them, and confirming the word with signs following.

The **Lord Jesus** is just the same today. The anointing is just the same. The Pentecostal experience is just the same, and we are to look for the same results as set forth in Luke's record of what happened in the days of the early church.

John the Baptist said concerning **Jesus**, "He shall baptize you with the **Holy Ghost**, and with **FIRE**." **God's** ministers are to be a flame of **FIRE**—a perpetual flame, a constant **FIRE**, a continual burning flame, burning and shining lights. **God** has nothing less for us than to be **FLAMES** of **FIRE**. We must have a living faith in **God**, a faith that **God's** great might and power may Burn in us until our whole life is energized by the power of **God**.

I realize that when the **Holy Ghost** comes, He comes to enable us to show forth **Jesus** Christ in all of His glory, to make Him known as the One who heals today as in the days of old. The Baptism in the Spirit is to enable us to preach as they did at the beginning, through the power of the **Holy Ghost** sent down from heaven and with the manifestation of the gifts of the Spirit. Oh, if we would only let the **Lord** work in us, melting us until a new order arises, moved with His compassion!

I was traveling from Egypt to Italy. **God** was wonderfully on that ship with me, and every hour I was conscious of His blessed presence. A man on the ship suddenly collapsed and his wife was terribly alarmed, and everybody else seemed to be. Some said that he was about to die. But I saw it was just a glorious opportunity for the power of **God** to be manifested. Oh, what it means to be a flame of **FIRE**, to be indwelt by the living Christ! We are in a week condition if we have to pray for power when an occasion like that comes, or if we have to wait until we feel a sense of His presence.

The **Lord's** promise was, "Ye shall receive power after

that the **Holy Ghost** is come upon you," and if we will believe, the power of **God** will always be manifested when there is a dire need. When you exercise your faith, you will discover that there is a greater power within us than there is in the world. Oh, to be awakened out of unbelief into a place of daring for **God** on the authority of His blessed Book!

So right there on board that ship, in the name of **Jesus** I rebuked the devil, and to the astonishment of the man's wife and the man himself, he was instantly healed. He said, "What is this? It is going all over me. I have never felt anything like this before." From the top of his head to the soles of his feet the power of **God** shook him. **God** has given us authority over all the power of the devil. Oh, that we may live in the place where we realize this always!

Christ, who is the express image of **God**, has come to our human weaknesses, to change us and to give us His divine likeness, to be partakers of His divine nature, so that by the power of His might we may not only overcome, but rejoice in the fact that we are more than conquerors. **God** wants you to know by experience what it means to be more than a conqueror.

The Baptism in the **Holy Spirit** has come for nothing less than to empower us, to give the very power that Christ Himself had, so that you, a yielded vessel, may continue the same type of ministry that He had when He walked this earth in the days of His flesh. He purposes that we should come behind in no gift. There are gifts of healing and the working of miracles, but we must apprehend these. There is the gift of faith by the same Spirit which we are to receive.

The greatest need in the world today is that we should be burning and shining lights to reflect the glory of Christ. We cannot do it with a cold indifferent experience, and we never shall. His servants are to be **FLAMES** of burning **FIRE**. Christ came that we might have life, and life more abundantly. And we are to give that life to others, to be ministers of the life and power and healing virtue of **Jesus** Christ wherever we go.

Some years ago I was in Ceylon. In one place the folk complained, "Four days is not much to give us." "No," I said, "but it will be a wonderful time." They said to me, "We are not reaching enough people." I said, "Can you have a meeting early in the morning, at eight o'clock?" They said they would. So I said, "Tell all the mothers who want their babies to be healed to come, and all the people over seventy to come, and after that we hope to give an address to the people to get them ready for the Baptism in the Spirit."

It would have done you good to see the four hundred mothers coming at eight o'clock in the morning with their babies, and then to see the hundred and fifty old people, with their white hair, coming to be healed. We need to have something more than smoke to touch the people; we need to be a burning **FIRE** for **God**. His ministers must be **FLAMES** of **FIRE**. In those days there were thousands out to hear the Word of **God**. I believe there were about three thousand persons crying for mercy at once in a meeting. It was an amazing and great sight.

From that first morning on the meetings grew to such an extent that I would estimate every time some 5,000 to 6,000 gathered; and I had to preach in a temperature of 110 degrees. Then I had to pray for these people who were sick. But I can tell you, a flame of **FIRE** can do anything. Things change in the **FIRE** of **God**.

This was Pentecost. But what moved me more than anything else was this: there were hundreds who tried to touch me, they were so impressed with the power of **God** that was present. And many testified that with the touch they were healed, it was not that there was any virtue in me—the people's faith was exercised as it was at Jerusalem when they said Peter's shadow would heal them.

You can receive something in three minutes that you can carry with you into glory. What do you want? Is anything too hard for **God**? **God** can meet you now. **God** sees inwardly, He knows all about you. Nothing is hidden from Him, and He can satisfy the soul and give you a spring of eternal blessing that will carry you through to the end.

FIRE FIRE FIRE

I believe there is a day coming greater than anything any of us have ever dreamed or imagined. This is the testing road. This is the place where your whole body must be covered with the wings of **God** that your nakedness shall not be seen. This is the thing that **God** is getting you ready for, the most wonderful thing your heart can conceive.

How can you get into it? First, "Ye have continued with me in my temptations." He had been in trials, **Jesus** had been in temptation. There is not one of us that is tempted beyond what He was. If a young man can be so pure that he cannot be tempted, he will never be fit to be made a judge, but **God** intends us to be so purified during these evil days that He can make us judges in the world to come.

If we can be tried, if we can be tempted on any line, **Jesus** said, "Ye are they which have continued with Me in My temptation." Have faith and **God** will keep you pure in the temptation. How shall we reach it? In Matt. 19:28, **Jesus** said, "Ye which have followed me in the regeneration when the Son of Man shall sit in the throne of His glory, ye also shall sit upon twelve thrones, judging the twelve tribes of Israel."

"Follow in regeneration" and every day is a regeneration; every day is a day of advancement; every day is a place of choice. Every day you find yourself in need of fresh consecration, faithfulness, commitment, and dedication. If you are in a place to yield **God** moves, you in the place of regeneration.

For years and years **God** has been making me appear to hundreds and thousands of people as a fool. I remember the day when He saved me and when He called me out. If there is a thing **God** wants to do today, He wants to be as real to you and me as He was to Abraham.

After I was saved I joined myself up to a very lively group of people who were full of a spirit of revival, and it was marvelous how **God** blest this gathering of believers. But then there came a Luke warmness and indifference amongst us, and **God** said to me as clearly as anything, "Come out."

 I obeyed and came out. The people said, "We cannot understand you. We need you now and you are leaving us." The Plymouth Brethren at that time were in a Conference. The Word of **God** was with them in power, the love of **God** was with them. Baptism by immersion was revealed to me, and when my friends saw me go into the water they said I was altogether wrong. But **God** had called me and I obeyed. The day came when I saw that the Brethren had dropped down to the letter, all letter, dry and barren.

At that time the Salvation Army was filled with love, filled with power, filled with zeal; every place a revival, and I joined up with them. For about six years the glory of **God** was there, and then the **Lord** said again, "Come out," and I am glad I came. The Salvation Army became a social movement and **God** has no place for a social movement. We are saved by regeneration, from glory to glory and the man who is going deeper with **God** has no time for social reforms.

God moved on, and at that time there were many people who were receiving the baptism of the **Holy Ghost** without signs. Those days were "days of heaven on earth." **God** unfolded the truth, showed the way of sanctification by the power of the blood of **Jesus** Christ, and I experienced the great inflow of the life of **God**.

I thank **God** for that, but **God** came along again and said, "Come out." I obeyed **God** and went with what they called the "tongues" people; they had further light that I needed. I saw **God** advancing every step I made, and I can see even in this Pentecostal work, except we see there is a real death yourself, **God** will say to us, "Come out."

Unless the present Pentecost movement wakes up to shake herself free from all the carnal worldly things and comes into a place of the divine-likeness with **God**, we will hear the voice of **God** once again say, "Come out" and He will give us something far better than what we now have.

I ask every one of you listening to the sound of my voice, will you hear the voice of **God** and come out? You ask, "What do you mean?" Everyone who is hungry for **God** knows without exception, there is only one word for Pentecost, and that is **FIRE**! If you are not ablaze you are not in the place were **God** can mightily use you. It is only the **FIRE** of **God** that burns up the entanglements of the world.

When we came into this new work **God** spoke to us by the Spirit and we knew we had to reach the place of absolute submission and cleansing, so that there would be nothing left. We were swept and garnished. Now, that was only the beginning, and if you have not made spiritual progress into that holy place of zeal, power, and compassion for **God**, we can truly say you have backslidden in heart. The backslider in heart is dead to **God's** fullness. He is not having fresh vision. The backslider in heart is not seeing the Word of **God** living and fresh every day.

You can put it down that a man is a backslider in heart if does not hate the sinful things of the world.

And if you have the applause of the world you do not having the approval of **God**. I do not know whether you will receive it or not but my heart burns with this message, "changing in the regeneration" for in this changing you will get a place in the kingdom to come where you shall be in authority; that place which **God** has prepared for us, that place which is beyond all human conception.

We can catch a glimpse of that glory, when we see how John worshipped the angel, and the angel said to him, "See thou do it not, for I am thy fellow-servant, of thy brethren the prophets." This angel is showing John the wonders of the glorious kingdom and in his glorified state, John thought he was the **Lord**. I wonder if we dare believe for this glorious place.

Let me close with these words: As sure as we have borne the image of the earthly, we shall also have the image of the heavenly. It means to us that everything of an earthly type has to cease, for the heavenly type is so wonderful in all of its purity. **God**, full of love, full of purity, full of power! No power only in the realm of purity! No open door into heaven only in the place of the conscience being void of sin between man and **God**, the heavens open only where the Spirit of the **Lord** is so leading, so that flesh has no power, but we will live in and by the Spirit. **God** bless you and prepare you for greater days.

A COAL OF FIRE

In the sixth of Isaiah we read of the prophet being in the presence of **God** and he found that even his lips were unclean and everything was unclean. But praise **God**, there is the same live coal for us today, the baptism of **FIRE**, the perfecting of the heart, the purifying of the mind, the regeneration of the spirit. How important it is that the **FIRE** of **God** shall touch our tongues.

In 1 John 4:1 we are told, "Beloved, believe not every spirit, but try the spirits whether they are of **God**." We are further told, "And every spirit that confesseth not that **Jesus** Christ is come in the flesh is not of **God**: and this is that spirit of antichrist, whereof ye have heard that it should come; and even now already is it in the world." From time to time as I have seen a person under the power of evil, or having a fit, I have said to the power of evil, or Satanic force that is within the possessed person, "Did **Jesus** Christ come in the flesh?"

And straightway they have answered, "No." They either say, "No," or hold their tongues, refusing altogether to acknowledge that the **Lord Jesus** Christ came in the flesh. It is then, remembering that further statement of John's, **"Greater is He that is in you than he that is in the world,"** that you can in the name of the **Lord Jesus**

Christ deal with the evil powers and command them to come out. We as Pentecostal people must know the tactics of the evil one and must be able to displace and dislodge him from his position.

I was preaching in Doncaster, England, at one time on the line of faith and a number of people were delivered. There was a man present who was greatly interested and moved by what he saw. He was suffering himself with a stiff knee and had yards and yards of flannel wound around it. After he got home he said to his wife, "I have taken in Wigglesworth's message and now I am going to act on it and get deliverance. Wife, I want you to be the audience." He took hold of his knee and said, "Come out, you devil, in the name of **Jesus**."

Then he said, "It is all right, wife." He took the yards and yards of flannel off and found he was all right without the bandage. The next night he went to the little Primitive Methodist Church where he worshiped. There were a lot of young people who were in bad plight there and Jack had a tremendous business delivering his friends through the name of **Jesus**. He had been given to see that a great many ills to which flesh is heir are nothing else but the operation of the enemy, but his faith had risen and he saw that in the name of **Jesus** there was a power that was more than a match for the enemy.

I arrived one night at Gottenberg in Sweden and was asked to hold a meeting there. In the midst of the meeting a man fell full length in the doorway. The evil spirit threw him down, manifesting itself and disturbing the whole meeting. I rushed to the door and laid hold of this man and cried out to the evil spirit within him, "Come out, you devil! In the name of **Jesus** we cast you out as an evil spirit." I lifted him up and said, "Stand on your feet and walk in the name of **Jesus**." I don't know whether anybody in the meeting understood me except the interpreter, but the devils knew what I said. I talked in English but these devils in Sweden cleared out. A similar thing happened in Christiania.

The devil will endeavor to fascinate through the eyes and through the mind. At one time there was brought to me a beautiful young woman who had been fascinated with some preacher, and just because he had not given her satisfaction on the line of courtship and marriage, the devil took advantage and made her fanatical and mad. They brought her 250 miles in that condition. She had previously received the Baptism in the Spirit.

You ask, "Is there any place for the enemy in one that has been baptized in the **Holy Ghost**?" Our only safety is in going on with **God** and in constantly being filled with the **Holy Ghost**. You must not forget Demas. He must have been baptized with the **Holy Ghost** for he appears to have been a right-hand worker with Paul, but the enemy got him to the place where he loved this present world and he dropped off. When they brought this young woman to me the evil power was immediately discerned and immediately I cast the thing out in the name of **Jesus**. It was a great joy to present her before all the people in her right mind again.

There is a life of perfect deliverance, and this is where **God** wants you to be. If I find my peace is disturbed on any line, I know it is the enemy who is trying to work. How do I know this? Because the **Lord** has promised to keep your mind in perfect peace when it is stayed on Him. Paul tells us to present our bodies a living sacrifice, holy, acceptable unto **God**, which is our reasonable service; the **Holy Spirit** breathes through him, "And be not conformed to this world; but be ye transformed by the renewing of your mind, that ye may prove what is that good, and acceptable, and perfect will of **God**."

He further tells us in Phil. 4, "Finally, brethren, whatsoever things are true, whatsoever things are honest, whatsoever things are just, whatsoever things are pure, what soever things are of good report; if there be any virtue, if there be any praise, think on these things." As we think about that which is pure, we become pure. As we think about that which is holy, we become holy. And as we think about our **Lord Jesus** Christ, we become like Him. We are changed into the likeness of the object on which our gaze is, fixed.

To discern spirits we must dwell with Him who is holy, and He will give the revelation and unveil the mask of satanic power in every area. In Australia I went to one place where there were disrupted and broken homes. The people were so deluded by the evil power of Satan that men had left their wives, and wives had left their husbands, and had gotten into relations with one another. That is the devil! May **God** deliver us from such evils in these days.

There is no one better than the companion **God** has given you. I have seen so many broken hearts and so many homes that have been wrecked. We need a real revelation of these evil seducing spirits which come in and fascinate by the eye and destroy lives, and bring the work of **God** into disrepute. But there is always flesh behind it. It is never clean; it is unholy, impure, satanic, devilish, and hell is behind it. If the enemy comes in to tempt you on any line like this, I beseech you to look instantly to the **Lord Jesus**. He can deliver you from any such satanic power. You must be separated in all areas if you are going to have faith.

The **Holy Ghost** will give us this gift of discerning of spirits if we desire it so that we may perceive by revelation this evil power which comes in to destroy. We can believe **God** to get this unction of the Spirit that will reveal these things unto us.

You will have people come to meetings who are spiritists. You must be able to deal with them. You can so deal with them that they will not have any power in the meetings. If you ever have Theosophists or Christian Scientists, you must be able to discern them and settle them. Never play with them; always clear them out. They are better with their own company always, unless they are willing to be delivered from the delusion they are in. Remember the warning of the **Lord Jesus**, "The thief cometh not, but for to steal, and to kill, and to destroy."

Before satan can bring his evil spirits there has to be an open door. Hear what the Scriptures say

"That wicked one toucheth him not" (1 John 5:18).

"The **Lord** shall preserve thee from all evil: He shall preserve thy soul" (Psa. 121:7). How does satan get an opening? When the saint ceases to seek after holiness, purity, righteousness, truth; when he ceases to pray, stops reading the Word and gives way to carnal appetites, then it is that Satan comes. So often sickness comes as a result of disobedience. David said, "Before I was afflicted, I went astray." Seek the **Lord** and He will sanctify every thought, every act, till your whole being is ablaze with holy purity and your one desire will be for Him who has created you in holiness. Oh, this holiness! Can we be made pure? We can. Every inbred sin must go.

God can cleanse away every evil thought. Can we have a hatred for sin and a love for righteousness? Yes, **God** will create within us a pure heart. He will take away the stony heart out of the flesh. He will sprinkle thee with clean water and thou shalt be cleansed from all thy filthiness. When will He do it? When you seek Him for such inward purity.

Smith - "Repeat in your heart often: "baptized with the Holy Ghost and FIRE, FIRE, FIRE!" All the unction, and weeping, and travailing comes through the baptism of FIRE, and I say to you and say to myself, purged and cleansed and filled with renewed spiritual power." "Who makes his ministers a flame of FIRE." Heb. 1:7]."

CHAPTER FIVE

WE MUST BE FILLED WITH FIRE

It is impossible to overestimate the importance of being filled with the Spirit. It is impossible for us to meet the conditions of the day, to walk in the light as He is in the light, to subdue kingdoms and work righteousness and bind the power of Satan unless we are filled with the **Holy Ghost**.

We read that in the early church they continued steadfastly in the apostles' doctrine and fellowship, and in breaking of bread, and in prayers. It is important for us also to continue steadfastly in these same things. For some years I was associated with the Plymouth Brethren. Now they were very strong on the Word, and were sound on water baptism, and they do not neglect the breaking of bread service, but have it every **Lord**'s Day morning as they had it in the early church. These people seem to have everything except the **FIRE**. They have the wood, but they need the intense hunger and then they would be all ablaze. Because they lack the **FIRE** of the **Holy Spirit** there is no life in their meetings.

One young man who attended their meetings received the Baptism with the speaking in other tongues as the Spirit gave utterance. The brethren were very upset about this and came to the **Father** and said to him, "You must take your son aside and tell him to cease." They did not want any disturbance. The **Father** told the son and said, "My boy, I have been attending this church for twenty years and have never seen anything of this kind.

We are established in the truth and do not want anything new. We won't have it." The son replied, "If that is **God's** plan I will obey, but somehow or other I don't think it is." As they were going home the horse stood still; the wheels were in deep ruts. The **Father** pulled at the reins but the horse did not move. He asked, "What do you think is up?" The son answered, "It has got established." **God** save us from becoming stationary.

God would have us to understand concerning spiritual gifts and to covet earnestly the best gifts, and also to enter into the more excellent way of the fruit of the Spirit. We must beseech **God** for these gifts. It is a serious thing to have the Baptism and yet be stationary; to live two days in the same spiritual plane is tragic. We must be willing to deny ourselves everything to receive the revelation of **God's** truth and to receive the fullness of the Spirit.

Only that will satisfy **God**, and nothing less must satisfy us. A young Russian received the **Holy Spirit** and was mightily endued with power from on High. Some sisters were anxious to know the secret of his power. The secret of his power was hunger and continuous waiting upon **God**. As the **Holy Ghost** filled him it seemed as though every breath became a prayer and so all his ministry was on an ever increasing position.

I know a man who was full of the **Holy Ghost** and would preach only when he knew that he was mightily unctioned by the power of **God**. He was asked to preach at a Methodist church. He was staying at the minister's house and he said, "You go on to church and I will follow."

The place was packed with people and this man did not turn up and the Methodist minister, becoming anxious, sent his little girl to inquire why he did not come. As she came to the bedroom door she heard him crying out three times, "I will not go." She went bark and reported that she heard the man say three times that he would not go.

The minister was troubled about it, but almost immediately after this the man came in, and, as he preached that night, the power of **God** was tremendously manifested. The preacher asked him, "Why did you tell my daughter that you were not coming?" He answered, "I know when I am filled. I am an ordinary man and I told the **Lord** that I dared not go and would not go until He gave me a fresh filling of the Spirit. The moment the glory filled me and overflowed I came to the meeting."

Yes, there is a power, a blessings, an assurance, a rest in

the presence of the **Holy Ghost**. You can feel His presence and know that you know He is with you. You need not spend an hour without this inner knowledge of His holy presence. With His power upon you there can be no failure. You are operating far above the natural realm at all the time.

"Ye know that ye were Gentiles, carried away unto these dumb idols, even as ye were led." This is the time of the Gentiles. When the Jews refused the blessings of **God** He scattered them, and He has grafted the Gentiles into the olive tree where the Jews were broken off.

There never has been a time when **God** has been so favorable to a people who were not a people. He. has brought in the Gentiles to carry out His purpose of preaching the gospel to all nations and to receive the power of the **Holy Ghost** to accomplish his mission in the earth. It is of the mercy of **God** that He has turned to the Gentiles and made us partakers of all the blessings that belong to the Jews; and here under this canopy of glory, because we believe, we get all the blessings of faithful Abraham.

"Wherefore I give you to understand, that no man speaking by the Spirit of **God** calleth **Jesus** accursed: and that no man can say that **Jesus** is the **Lord**, but by the **Holy Ghost**." There are many evil, deceiving spirits sent forth in these last days who endeavor to rob office of the revelation of **Jesus** and His **Lord**ship and of His rightful place.

Many are opening the doors to these latest devils, such as New Theology and New Thought and Christian

Science. These evil cults deny the fundamental truths of **God's** Word. They all deny eternal punishment and all deny the deity of **Jesus** Christ. You will never see the Baptism of the **Holy Ghost** come upon a man who accepts these errors. Neither will you see a devout Romanist receive.

They put Mary in the place of the **Holy Ghost**. I would like you to produce a devout Romanist who knows that he is saved. No man can know he is saved by works. If you ever speak to a devout Romanist you will know that he is ignorant of the new birth. Another thing, you will never find a Mormon baptized in the **Holy Ghost**; nor a member of any other cult that does not put the **Lord Jesus** Christ pre-eminent above all.

The all important thing is to make **Jesus Lord**. Men can grow lopsided by emphasizing the truth of divine healing. Man can get wrong by all the time preaching on water baptism. But we never go wrong in exalting the **Lord Jesus** Christ, giving Him the preeminent place and magnifying Him as both **Lord** and Christ, yes, as very **God** of very **God**. As we are filled with the **Holy Ghost** our one desire is to magnify Him. We need to be filled with the Spirit to get the full revelation of the **Lord Jesus** Christ.

God's command is for us to be filled with the Spirit. We are no good if we have only a full cup; we need to have an overflowing cup all the time. It is a tragedy not to live in the fullness of overflowing. See that you never live below the overflowing tide.

"Now there are diversities of gifts but the same Spirit."

Smith Wigglesworth When the FIRE Fell

Every manifestation of the Spirit is given that we might "profit withal." When the **Holy Spirit** is moving in an assembly and His gifts are in operation, everyone will receive profit. I have seen some who have been terribly confused. They believe in gifts, in prophecy, and they use these gifts apart from the power of the **Holy Ghost**.

We must look to the **Holy Spirit** to show us the use of the gifts, what they are for, and when to use them, so that we may never use them without the power of the **Holy Ghost**. I do not know of anything which is so awful today as people using a gift without the power. **God** save us from doing it.

A man who is filled with the **Holy Ghost**, while he may not be conscious of having any gift of the Spirit, can have the gifts made manifest through him.

I have gone to many places to help and have found that under the unction of the **Holy Spirit** many wonderful things have happened in the midst when the glory of the **Lord** was upon the people. Any man who is filled with **God** and filled with His Spirit might at any moment have any of the nine gifts made manifest through him without knowing that he has a gift.

Sometimes I have wondered whether it was better to be always full of the **Holy Ghost** and to see signs and wonders and miracles without any consciousness of possessing a gifts or whether it was better to know one has a gift. If you have received the gifts of the Spirit and they have been blessed, you should never under any circumstances use them without the power of **God** upon you causing the gift to flow through you.

Some have used the prophetic gift without the holy touch, and they have come into the realm of the natural, and it has brought ruin, caused dissatisfaction, broken hearts, and upset assemblies. Do not seek the gifts unless you are purposed to abide in the **Holy Spirit**. They should be manifested only in the power of the **Holy Spirit**.

The **Lord** will allow you to be very drunk in His presence, but sober among people. I like to see people so filled with the Spirit that they are drunk like the 120 on the Day of Pentecost, but I don't like to see people drunk in the wrong place. That is what troubles us, somebody being drunk in a place of worship where a lot of people come in that know nothing about the Word. If you allow yourself to be drunk there you send people away; they look at you instead of seeing **God**. They condemn the whole thing because you have not been sober at the right time.

Paul writes, "For whether we be beside ourselves, it is to **God**: or whether we be sober, it is for your cause" (2 Cor. 5:13). You can be beside yourself. You can go a bit further than being drunk. You can dance if you will do it at the right time. So many things are commendable when all the people are in the Spirit.

Many things are very foolish if the people round about you are not in the Spirit. We must be careful not to have a good time at the expense of somebody else. When you have a good time you must see that the spiritual conditions in the place lend themselves to help you and that the people are coming in line with you. Then you will find it always a blessing.

Smith Wigglesworth When the FIRE Fell

While it is right to covet earnestly the best gifts, you must recognize that the all-important thing is to be filled with the power of the **Holy Ghost** Himself. You will never have trouble with people who are filled with the power of the **Holy Ghost**. But you will have a lot of trouble with people who have the gifts and have no power. The **Lord** wants us to come behind in no gift, but at the same time He wants us to be so filled with the **Holy Ghost** that it will be the **Holy Spirit** manifesting Himself through the gifts.

Where the glory of **God** alone is desired, you can look for every needed gift to be made manifest. To glorify **God** is better than to idolize gifts. We prefer the Spirit of **God** to any gift; but we can look for the tri-unity of **God** to be manifested, different gifts by the same Spirit, different administrations but the sane **Lord**, and diversities of operation but the same **God** working all in all. Can you conceive of what it will mean for our Triune **God** to be manifesting Himself in His fullness in our assemblies?

You can watch a great locomotive boiler as it is filled with steam. You can see the engine letting off some of the steam as it remains stationary. It looks as though the whole thing might explode. You can see saints like that. They start to scream, but that is not to edification. But when the locomotive moves on, it serves the purpose for which it was built, and pulls along large train cars with it. It is wonderful to be filled with the power of the **Holy Ghost**, and for Him to serve His own purposes through us.

Through our lips divine utterances flow, our hearts

rejoice, and our tongue are glad. It is an inward power within which is manifested in an outward expression. **Jesus** Christ is glorified, as your faith in Him is quickened, from within you there will flow rivers of living water. The **Holy Spirit** will pour through you like a great river of life and thousands will be blessed because you are a yielded channel through whom the Spirit may flow.

The most important thing, the one thing that counts, is to see that we are filled with the **Holy Spirit**, filled to overflowing. Anything less than this is displeasing to **God**. We are commanded by **God** to be filled with the Spirit, and in the measure, you fall short of this you will not be able to fulfill all of the plan of **God**.

The **Lord** would have us moving on from faith to faith, from glory to glory, from fullness to overflowing. It is not good for us to be ever thinking in the past tense, but we should be moving on to the place where we dare believe **God**. He has declared that after the **Holy Ghost** is come upon us we shall have power. I believe there is an avalanche of power from **God** to be apprehended if we will but catch the vision, and believe his word.

Paul wrote at one time, "I will now come to visions and revelations." **God** has put us in a place where He expects us to have His latest revelation, the revelation of that marvelous fact, CHRIST IN US, and what this really means. We can apprehend Christ fully only as we are filled and overflowing with the Spirit of **God**. Our only safeguard from dropping back into our natural mind from which we can never get anything, is to be filled and yet filled again with the Spirit of **God** and to be taken on to visions and revelations on a new level.

The reason why I emphasize the importance of the fullness of the **Holy Ghost** is that I want to get you beyond all human plans and thoughts into the fullness of vision, into the full revelation of the **Lord Jesus** Christ. Do you want rest? It is in **Jesus**. Do you want to be saved from everything the devil is bringing up in these last times? Receive and continue in the fullness of the **Holy Ghost**, and He will be ever revealing to you that all you need for all times is in Christ **Jesus** your **Lord**.

I desire to emphasize the importance of the Spirit's ministration and of the manifestation of the Spirit which is given to every man to profit withal. As you yield to the Spirit of the **Lord** He has power over your intellect, over your heart, and over your voice. The **Holy Spirit** has power to unveil Christ and to project the vision of Christ upon the canvas of your mind, and then He uses your tongue to glorify and magnify Him in a way that you could never do apart from the Spirit's power.

Never say that when you are filled with the **Holy Ghost** you are "obliged" to do this or that. When people say that they are "obliged" to do this or that I know it is not the Spirit of **God**, but their own spirit moving them on to do that which is unseemly and unprofitable. Lots of people spoil meetings because they scream. If you want to do that kind of thing you had better get into some cellar. That is not to edification. I believe that, when the Spirit of **God** is upon you and moving you to speak as He gives utterance, it will always be to edification.

But don't spoil the gathering because when you ought to

stop you go on. Who spoils the meeting? The man who starts in the Spirit and finishes in the flesh. Nothing is more lovely than prayer, but a prayer meeting is killed if you will go on and on in your own soul when the Spirit of **God** is finished with you.

You say as you come from some meetings, "That was a lovely message if the preacher only had stopped half an hour before he did." Learn to cease immediately the unction of the Spirit lifts. The **Holy Ghost** is jealous. Your body is the temple, the office of the **Holy Ghost**, but He does not fill the temple for human glorification, but only for the glory of **God**. You have no license to continue beyond a "Thus saith the **Lord**."

There is another side to this. **God** would have the gathering as free as possible, and you must not put your hand upon the working of the Spirit, or it will surely turn sourer. You must be prepared to allow a certain amount of extravagance in young and newly baptized souls. You must remember that when you were brought into this life of the Spirit you had as many extravagances as anybody, but you have now become somewhat more mature.

It is a pity that some do get to sober, for they are not where they were in the early days. We must look to **God** for wisdom that we do not interfere or dampen the Spirit or quench the power of **God** when it is manifested in our meetings. If you want to have an assembly full of life you must have an assembly full of manifestation. Nobody will come if there is no manifestation. We need to look to **God** for special grace that we do not move back to looking at things from a natural viewpoint.

Smith Wigglesworth When the FIRE Fell

The preacher, after he loses his unction, should inwardly repent and get right with **God** and get the unction back. We are no good without the unction of the Spirit of **God**. If you are filled with the grace of **God** you will not be judging everybody in the assembly, and you will not be easily frightened at what is happening. You will have a heart to believe all things, and to believe that though there may be some extravagances, the Spirit of **God** will take control of things and will see that the **Lord Jesus** Christ Himself is exalted, glorified, and revealed to hungry hearts that desire to know Him. The **Lord** would have us wise unto that which is good and simple concerning evil, free from distrust, entering a divine likeness to **Jesus** that dares believe that **God** Almighty will surely watch over all. Hallelujah!

The **Holy Ghost** is the One who magnifies the **Lord Jesus** Christ, the One who gives illumination of Him. If you are filled with the **Holy Ghost**, it is impossible to keep your tongue still. Talk about a dumb baptized soul! It is not to be found in the Scriptures or outside of the Scriptures. We are filled with the Spirit in order that we may magnify the **Lord**, and there should be no meeting in which the saints do not glorify, magnify, praise, and worship the **Lord** in Spirit and in truth.

I would like to give one word of caution, for failure often comes through our not recognizing the fact that we are always in the body. We will need our bodies as long as we live. But our body is to be used and controlled by the Spirit of **God**. We are to present our bodies, holy and acceptable unto **God**, which is our reasonable service. Every member of our body must be so sanctified that it works in harmony with the Spirit of **God**. Our very eyes must be sanctified. **God** hates the winking of the eye. From the day that I read in the Proverbs what **God** had to say about the winking of the eye (Prov. 6:13 and 10:10) I have never winked. I desire that my eyes may be so sanctified that they can always be used for the **Lord**. The Spirit of **God** will bring within us a compassion for souls that will be seen in our very eyes.

God has never changed the order of things, first there comes the natural, and then the spiritual. For instance, when it is on your heart to pray, you begin in the natural and your second word will probably be under the power of the Spirit. You begin and **God** will end. It is the same in giving forth utterances under the Spirit's power.

You feel the moving of the Spirit within, and you begin to speak and the Spirit of **God** will give forth utterance. Thousands have missed wonderful blessings because they have not had faith to move out and begin in the natural, in faith that the **Lord** would take them into the realm of the supernatural. When you receive the **Holy Ghost** you receive **God's** Gift, in whom are all the gifts of the Spirit.

Paul counsels Timothy to stir up the gift that was within. You have power to stir up **God's** Spirit within you. The way you stir up the gift within you is by beginning in faith, and then He gives forth what is needed for the occasion. You will never begin if you think you have to be full of **God**. When we yield to timidity and fear we simply yield to Satan. Satan. Whispers, "It is all self." He is a liar. I have learned this, if the Spirit of **God** is stirring me up, I have no hesitation in beginning to speak in tongues, and the Spirit of **God** gives me utterance and gives me the interpretation. I find that every time I yield to the **Lord** on this order I get a divine touch, I get a leading thought from the Spirit of **God** and the meeting is moved into the realm of faith.

You attend a meeting in faith, believing that the **Lord** is going to meet you there. But perhaps the evangelist is not in harmony with **God**. The people in the meeting are not getting what **God** wants. The **Lord** knows it. He knows His people are hungry. What happens? He will take perhaps the smallest vessels and put His power upon them. As they yield to the Spirit they break forth in a tongue.

 Another yields to the Spirit and there comes forth the interpretation. The **Lord**'s church has to be fed, and the **Lord** will take this means of speaking to His people. Pentecostal people cannot be satisfied with the natural message. They are in touch with heavenly things and cannot be satisfied with anything less. They feel when there is something lacking in a meeting, and they look to **God** and He supplies that which is lacking.

When a man is filled with the Spirit he really has very little understanding of what he has. We are so limited in our understanding of what we have received. The only way we can know the power that has been given to us is through the ministration and manifestation of the Spirit of **God**. Do you think that Peter and John knew what they had when they went up to the temple to pray? They were limited in thought and limited in their expression. The nearer we get to **God** the more conscious we are of the poverty of our human soul and we cry with Isaiah, "I am undone, I am unclean." But the **Lord** will bring the precious blood and the flaming coals for cleansing and refining and send us out to labor for Him empowered by His Spirit.

God has sent forth this outpouring that we may all be brought into a revelation of our son ship - that we are sons of **God**, men of power, that we are to be like the **Lord Jesus** Christ, that we are to have the powers of son ship, the power to lay hold of that which is weak and to quicken it. The Baptism of the Spirit is to make us sons of **God** with power. We shall be conscious of our human limits, but we shall not limit the Holy One who has come to dwell within.

We must believe that since the **Holy Ghost** has come upon us we are indeed sons of **God** with power. Never say that you can't. All things are possible to them that believe. Launch out into the deep and believe that **God** has His all for you, and that you can do all things through Him who strengthens you.

Peter and John knew that they had been in the upper room, they had felt the glory. That they had been given divine utterances. They had seen conviction on the people. They knew that they had come into a wonderful thing. They know that what they had would be ever increasing and that it would be ever needful to cry, "Enlarge the vessel that the **Holy Ghost** may have more room within."

They knew that all the old things were moved away and they had entered into increasing and ever increasing knowledge of **God**, and that it was their Master's wish that they should be filled with the Spirit of **God** and with power every day and every hour. The secret of power is the unveiling of Christ, the all-powerful One within, the revelation of **God** who comes to abide within us.

As they looked upon the crippled man at the Beautiful Gate they were filled with compassion. They were prompted by the Spirit to stop and speak with him. They said to the lame man, "Look on us." It was **God's** plan that the man should open his eyes with expectation. Peter said, "Of silver and gold we have none. But we have something, and we will give it to you. We don't know what it is, but we give it to you. It is all in the name of **Jesus**." And then began the ministry of **God**.

You begin in faith and then you see what will happen. It is hidden from us at the beginning, but as we have faith in **God** He will come forth. The coming forth of the power is not of us but of **God**. There is no limit to what He will do. It is all in a nutshell as you believe **God**. And so Peter said, "Such as I have I give to thee: in the name of **Jesus** Christ of Nazareth rise up and walk." And the man who had been in that way for forty years stood up, and began to leap, and entered into the temple walking and leaping and praising **God**.

"For to one is given by the Spirit the word of wisdom." I want you to keep in mind the importance of never expecting the gifts of the Spirit apart from the power of the Spirit. In coveting the best gifts, covet to be so full of **God** and His glory that the gifts in manifestation will always glorify Him.

We do not know all and we cannot know all that can be

brought forth in the manifestation of the word of wisdom. One word of wisdom from **God**, one flash of light on the Word of **God**, is sufficient to save us from a thousand pitfalls. People have built without a word from **God**, they have bought things without a word from **God**, and they have been ensnared. They have lacked that word of wisdom which will bring them into **God's** plan for their lives. I have been in many places where I have needed a word from **God** and this has been my place of refuge.

I will give you one instance. There is one thing I am very grateful to the **Lord** for, and that is that He has given me grace not to have a desire for money. The love of money is a great hindrance to many; and many a man is crippled in his ministry because he lets his heart run after financial matters. I was walking out one day when I met a godly man who lived opposite me and he said, "My wife and I have been talking together about selling our house and we feel constrained to sell it to you." As we talked together he persuaded me to buy his place, and before we said good-by I told him that I would take it.

We always make big mistakes when we are in a hurry. I told my wife what I had promised, and she said, "How will you manage it?" I told her that I had managed things so far, but I did not know how I was going to get through this. I somehow knew that I was out of divine order. But when a fellow gets out of divine order it seems that the last person he goes to is **God**.

I ended up relying on an architect to help me, but that scheme fell through. I turned to my relations and I ended up with mud on my face as one after another turned me down. I tried my friends and managed no better. My wife said to me, "Thou hast never been to **God** Yet." What could I do?

I have a certain place in our house where I go to pray. I have been there very often. As I went I said, "**Lord**, if You will get me out of this mess, I will never trouble You on this line again." As I waited on the **Lord** He just gave me one word. It seemed a ridiculous thing, but it was the wisest counsel. There is divine wisdom in every word He speaks. I came down to my wife, saying, "What do you think? The **Lord** has told me to go to Brother Webster." I said, "It seems very ridiculous, for he is one of the poorest men I know." He was the poorest man I knew, but he was also the richest man I knew, for he knew **God**. My wife said, "Do What **God** says, and it will be right."

I went off at once to see him, and he said as he greeted me, "Smith, what brings you so early?" I answered, "The word of **God**." I said to him, "About three weeks ago I promised to buy a house of a man, and I am short 100 pounds ($500). I have tried to get this money, but somehow I seem to have missed **God**." "How is it," he asked, "that you have come to me only now?"

I answered, "Because I went to the **Lord** about it only last night." "Well," he said, "it is a strange thing; three weeks ago I had 100 pounds. For years I have been putting money into a co-operative system and three weeks ago I had to go and draw 100 pounds out. I hid it under the mattress. Come with me and you shall have it. Take it. I hope it will bring as great a blessing to you as it has been a trouble to me." I had a word from **God**, and all my troubles were ended.

This has been multiplied in a hundred ways since that time. If I had been filled with the **Holy Ghost**, I would not have bought that house and would not have had all that pressure. I believe the **Lord** wants to loose us from things of earth. But I am ever grateful for that word from **God**. There have been times in my life when I have been in great crises and under great weight of intercession.

 I have gone to the meeting without the knowledge of what I would say, but somehow or other **God** would give by the Spirit some word of wisdom, just what some souls in that meeting needed. As we look to **God** His mind will be made known, and His revelation and His word of wisdom will be forth coming.

"If thou shalt confess with thy mouth JESUS AS LORD, and shalt believe in thine heart that God hath raised him from the dead, thou shalt be saved" **(Romans 10:9).**

"For TO THIS END Christ died and lived again, THAT HE MIGHT BE LORD of both the dead and the living" (Romans 14:9).

Smith - "I know that **God's** word is sufficient. One word from Him can change a nation. His word is from everlasting to everlasting. It is through the entrance of this everlasting Word, this incorruptible seed, that we are born again, and come into this wonderful salvation. Man cannot live by bread alone but must live by every word that proceeded out of the mouth of **God**. This is the food of faith. "Faith cometh by hearing, and hearing by the Word of **God**.".

CHAPTER SIX

WHOLE BODY IS A FLAME WITH GOD

God wants to flow through you in marvelous power with divine utterance and grace, until your whole body is a flame of **FIRE**. **God** intends each soul in Pentecost to be a live wire. So many people who have been baptized with the **Holy Ghost** came in because there was a movement, but so many of them have become monuments, and you cannot move them.

The Baptism in the Spirit should be an ever-increasing enlargement of grace. Jump in, stop in, and never come out; for this is the Baptism which is meant to be that we are lost in it, where you only know one thing, and that is the desire of **God** at all times. O **Father**, grant unto us a real look into the glorious liberty that Thou hast designed for the children of **God** who are delivered from this

91

present evil world, separated, sanctified, and made meet for Thy use; whom Thou hast designed to be filled with all Thy fullness!

Nothing has hurt me so much as this: to see so-called believers have so much unbelief in them that it is hard to move them. Everything is possible to them that believe. **God** will not fail to fulfill His Word, wherever you are. Suppose that all the people in the world did not believe, that would make no difference to **God** or his Word. It would be the same. You cannot alter **God's** Word. It is from everlasting to everlasting, and they who believe in it shall be like Mount Zion which cannot be moved.

God heals by the power of His Word. But the most important thing is this: Are you saved? Do you know the **Lord**? Are you prepared to meet **God**? You may be an invalid as long as you live, but you may be saved by the power of **God**. You may have a strong, healthy body, but may go straight to hell because you know nothing of the grace of **God** and salvation. Thank **God**, I was saved in a moment, the moment I believed. And **God** will do the same for you.

The Spirit of **God** would have us understand there is nothing that can interfere stop us getting into **God's** perfect blessing except our unbelief. Unbelief is a terrible hindrance. As soon as we are willing to allow the **Holy Ghost** to have His way, we shall find great things will happen all the time. But oh, how much of our own human reason we have to get rid of, our carnality!

How much human planning we have to become to be

divorced from! What would happen right now if everyone believed **God**? I love the thought that **God** the **Holy Ghost** wants to emphasize truth. If we will only yield ourselves to the divine plan, He is right here to do great things, and to fulfill the promise in Joel 2.21, "Fear not, O land; be glad and rejoice: for the **Lord** will do great things."

How many of us truly believe the Word of **God**? It is easy to quote it, but it is more important to believe it than to quote it. It is very easy for me to quote, "Now are we the sons of **God**," but it is more important for me to know whether I am a son of **God**, When the Son of **God** was on the earth He was recognized by the people who heard Him. "Never man spake like this man."

His word was with power, and that word came to pass. Sometimes you have quoted, "Greater is He that is in you, than he that is in the world," and you could not tell just where to find it. But, brother, is it so? Can demons remain in your presence? You have to be greater than demons. Disease cannot lodge in your body when you are in fellowship with **God**. You have to be greater than the disease. Can anything in the world stand against you and resist you? It needs to be a fact a reality in your heart that Greater Is He That Is in You than He That Is in the World?

Have faith in the fact that Christ dwells in you, and dare to act in harmony with that glorious truth. Christ said, "Have faith in **God**. For verily I say unto you, That whosoever shall say unto this mountain, Be thou removed, and be thou cast into the sea; and shall not doubt in his heart, but shall believe that those things which he saith shall come to pass, he shall have whatsoever he saith."

If you have been begotten of the Word and the Word is in you, the life of the Son is in you, and **God** wants you to fully believe this reality. He says to you, "What things soever ye desire, when ye pray, believe that ye receive them, and ye shall have them."

A Flaming FIRE

Stephen was a man full of faith, **FIRE** and of the **Holy Ghost**. **God** declares it. **God** so manifested Himself in Stephen's body that he became an epistle of truth, known and read of all. Full of faith! Such men never talk doubt. You never hear them say, "I wish it could be so; or if it is **God's** will." No IFS. They KNOW. You never hear them say, "Well, it does not always work." They say, "It is absolutely to be." They laugh at impossibilities and cry, "It shall be done!" A man full of faith hopes against hope. He shouts while the walls are up and they come down while he shouts! **God** has this faith for us in Christ. We must be careful that no unbelief is found in us, no wavering.

"Stephen, full of faith and power, did great wonders and miracles among the people." The **Holy Ghost** could do mighty things through him because he believed **God**, and **God** is with the man who dares to believe His Word. All things were possible because of the **Holy Ghost**'s presence in Stephen's body. He was full of the **Holy Ghost** so **God** could fulfill His purposes through him. When a child of **God** is filled with the **Holy Ghost**, the Spirit that ever liveth maketh intercession through them for the saints according to the will of **God**. He fills us with longings and desires until we are in a place of fervency as of molten metal in a **FIRE**.

What to do we know not within our flesh, but when we are in this place the **Holy Ghost** begins to do the **Father**'s will. When the **Holy Ghost** has full liberty in our bodies He will pray through us according to the will of **God**. Such prayers are always heard. Such praying is always answered; it is never empty of result. When we are praying in the **Holy Ghost**, faith is in evidence and as a result the power of **God** can be manifested in our midst.

When there arose certain of the various synagogues to dispute with Stephen they were not able to resist the wisdom and the Spirit by which He spoke. When we are filled with the **Holy Ghost** we will have wisdom beyond man's intellect. Praise **God**! One night I was entrusted with a meeting and I was zealous of my position before **God**. I wanted approval from the **Lord**. I see that **God** wants men full of the **Holy Ghost**, with divine ability, filled with life, a flaming **FIRE**. In this meeting a young man stood up, a pitiful object, with a face full of sorrow.

I said, "What is it, young man?"

He said he was unable to work, and that he could scarcely walk. He said, "I am so helpless. I have consumption and a weak heart, and my body is full of pain."

I said, "I will pray for you." I said to the people, "As I pray for this young man, you look at his face and you will see it change."

As I prayed his face changed. I said to him, "Go out and run a mile and come back to the meeting."

He came back and said, "I can now breathe freely."

The meetings were continuing and I missed him. After a few days I saw him again in the meeting. I said, "Young man, tell the people what **God** has done for you." "Oh," he said, "I have been to work. I bought some papers and I have made $4.50."

Praise **God**, this wonderful River of salvation never runs dry. You can take a drink from this wonderful river. It is a river that is running deep and there is plenty for all.

In a meeting a man rose and said, "Will you touch me, I am in a terrible way. I have a family of children, and through an accident in the coal mine I have had no work for two years. I cannot open my hands."

I was full of compassion for this poor man and something happened which had never come before. We are in the infancy of this wonderful outpouring of the **Holy Spirit** and there is so much more for us.

I put out my hand, and before my hands reached his, his

hands were loosed and made perfectly free. I see that Stephen, full of faith and of power, did great wonders and miracles among the people. This same **Holy Ghost** filling is for us, and good things will be accomplished if we are filled with His Spirit. **God** will grant it. He declares that the desires of the righteous shall be granted.

Stephen was an ordinary man made extraordinary in **God**. We may be very ordinary, but **God** wants to make us extraordinary in the **Holy Ghost**. **God** is ready to touch and to transform you right now.

Once a woman rose in the meeting asking for prayer. I prayed for her and she was healed. She cried out, "It is a miracle! It is a miracle! It is a miracle!" That is what **God** wants to do for us all the time. As soon as we get free in the **Holy Ghost** something will happen. Let us pursue the best things and let **God** have His way in our lives.

All that sat in the council looked steadfastly on Stephen and saw his face as it had been the face of an angel. It was worth being filled with the **Holy Ghost** for that. The Spirit breaking through. There is a touch of the Spirit where the light of **God** will literally radiate from our faces.

The seventh chapter of Acts is the profound prophetic utterance that the Spirit spoke through this holy man. The word of **God** flowed through the lips of Stephen in the form of divine prophecy so that they who heard these things were cut to the heart. But he, being full of the **Holy Ghost**, looked up steadfastly into heaven, and saw the glory of **God**, and **Jesus** standing on the right hand of

God, and said, "Behold I see the heavens opened, and the Son of man standing on the right hand of **God**."

Right to the last Stephen was full of the **Holy Ghost**. He saw **Jesus** standing at the right hand of **God** the **Father**. In another part we read of **Jesus** seated at the right hand of **God**. That is His place of authority. But here we see that He arose. He was so keenly interested in that martyr Stephen. May the **Lord** open our eyes to see **Jesus** and to know that He is deeply interested in all that concerns us. He is touched with the feeling of our infirmities.

All things are naked and open unto the eyes of Him with whom we have to do. That asthma that is attacking you, He knows. That rheumatism afflicting you, He knows. That pain in the back of your head, those aching feet, He knows. He wants to loose every captive and to set you free just as He has set me free. I do not know that I have a body today. I am free of every human ailment, absolutely free. Christ has redeemed us. He has power over all the power of the enemy and has fought and won the battle for our great victory. Will you have it? It is yours, and it is a perfect redemption.

They stoned Stephen, who called upon **God** and said, "**Lord Jesus**, receive my spirit." And he kneeled down, and cried with a loud voice, "**Lord**, lay not this sin to their charge." And when he had said this he fell asleep. Stephen was not only filled with faith but he was also filled with love as he prayed just as his Master prayed, "**Father**, forgive them."

It is **God's** thought to make us a new creation, with all

the old things passed away and all things within us truly of **God**, to bring in a new divine order, a perfect love and an unlimited faith. Will you have it? Redemption is free. Arise in the activity, the operation, and the power of faith and **God** will heal you as you arise. Only believe and receive in faith all that **God** has promised you. Stephen, full of faith and of the **Holy Ghost**, did great signs and wonders. May **God** bless us with this revelation of his will and fill us full of His **Holy Spirit**. And through the power of the **Holy Ghost** reveal to us Christ in us.

The **Holy Ghost** of **God** will always reveal the **Lord Jesus** Christ. Serve Him, love Him, be filled with Him. It is lovely to hear Him as He makes Himself known to us. He is the same yesterday, today and forever. He is willing to fill us with the **Holy Ghost** and faith just as He filled Stephen.

"Have you received the Holy Ghost since you believed?" "Are you filled with divine power?"

This is the heritage of the Church, to be so endued with power that **God** can lay His hand upon any member at any time to do His perfect will. There is no stopping the Spirit-filled life: we begin at the Cross, the place of ridicule, terrible suffering, shame, and death, and that very death brings the power of resurrection life; and, being filled with the **Holy Spirit**, we go on "from glory to glory."

 Let us not forget that possessing the Baptism in the **Holy Spirit**, means there must be an "ever-increasing" holiness. How the Church needs divine unction—**God's** presence and power so manifested that the world will know it is **God** in us. The people know when the tide is flowing; they also know when it is ebbing.

The necessity that seven men be chosen for the position of "serving tables" was very evident. The disciples knew that these seven men were men ready for active service, and so they chose them. In the 5th verse, we read: "And the saying pleased the whole multitude, and they chose Stephen, a man full of faith and of the **Holy Ghost**, and Philip."

There were others, of course, but Stephen and Philip stand out most prominently in the Scriptures. Philip was a man so filled with the **Holy Ghost** that a revival always followed wherever he went. Stephen was a man so filled with divine power, that although serving tables might have been all right in the minds of the other disciples, yet, **God** had a greater vision for him—a baptism of **FIRE**, of power and divine unction, that took him on and on to the conclusion of his life, until he saw right into the open heavens.

Had we been there with the disciples at that time, I believe we should have heard them saying to each other, "Look here! Neither Stephen nor Philip are doing the work we called them to. If they do not attend to business, we shall have to get someone else!" That was the carnal way of thinking, but divine order is far above our fleshly planning. When we please **God** in our daily service, we shall always find in operation the fact "that everyone who is faithful in little, **God** will make faithful in much."

We have such an example right here—a man chosen to "serve tables," having such a revelation of the mind of Christ and of the depth and height of **God**, that there was no stopping in his experience, but a going forward with leaps and bounds. Beloved, there is a race to be run, there is a crown to be won; we cannot stand still! I say unto you, be vigilant! Be vigilant! "Let no man take thy crown!"

God has privileged us in Christ **Jesus** to live above the ordinary human plane of life. Those who want to be ordinary, and live on a lower plane, can do so; but as for me, I will not! For the same unction, the same zeal, the same **Holy Ghost** power is at our command as was at the command of Stephen and the apostles.

We have the same **God** that Abraham had, that Elijah had, and we need not come behind in any gift or grace. We may not possess the gifts, as abiding gifts, but as we are full of the **Holy Ghost** and divine unction, it is possible, when there is need, for **God** to manifest every gift of the Spirit through us. As I have already said, I do not mean by this that we should necessarily possess the gifts permanently, but there should be a manifestation of the gifts as **God** may choose to use us.

This ordinary man Stephen became mighty under the **Holy Ghost** anointing, until he stands supreme, in many ways, among the Apostles—"And Stephen full of faith and power, did great wonders and miracles among the people." As we go deeper in **God**, He enlarges our conception and places before us a wide-open door; and I am not surprised that this man chosen to "serve tables" was afterwards called to a higher plane. "What do you mean?" you may ask. "Did he quit this service?" No! But he was lost in the power of **God**.

He lost sight of everything in the natural, and steadfastly fixed his gaze upon **Jesus**, "the author and finisher of our faith," until he was transformed into a shining light in the kingdom of **God**, Oh that we might be awakened to believe His word, to understand the mind of the Spirit, for there is an inner place of whiteness and purity where we can "see **God**."

Stephen was just as ordinary a man as you and I, but he was in the place where **God** could so move upon him that he, in turn, could move all before him. He began in a most humble place, and ended in a blaze of glory. Beloved, dare to believe Christ!

As you go on in this life of the Spirit, you will find that the devil will begin to get restless and there will be a stir in the synagogue; it was so with Stephen. Any amount of people may be found in the "synagogue," who are very proper in a worldly sense—always correctly dressed, the elite of the land, welcoming into the church everything but the power of **God**. Let us read what **God** says about them:

"Then there arose certain in the synagogue, which is called the Synagogue of the Libertines, and Cyrenians, and Alexandrians ... disputing with Stephen, and they were not able to resist the wisdom and the spirit by which he spake."

"The Libertines" could not stand the truth of **God**. With these opponents, Stephen found himself in the same predicament as the blind man whom **Jesus** healed. As soon as the blind man's eyes were opened they shut him out of the synagogue. They will not have anybody in the "synagogue" with their eyes open; as soon as you receive spiritual eyesight, out you go!

These Libertines, Cyrenians, and Alexandrians, rose up full of wrath in the very place where they should have been full of the power of **God**, full of love divine, and reverence for the **Holy Ghost**; they rose up against Stephen, this man "full of the **Holy Ghost**." Beloved, if there is anything in your life that in any way resists the power of the **Holy Ghost** and the entrance of His word into your heart and life, drop on your knees and CRY ALOUD for mercy! When the Spirit of **God** is brooding over your heart's door, do not resist Him but open your heart to the touch of **God**, There is a resisting "unto blood" striving against sin, and there is a resisting of the **Holy Ghost** that will drive you into sin.

Stephen spoke with divine **Holy Ghost** wisdom; where he was, things began to move. You will find that there is always a moving when the **Holy Spirit** has control. These people were brought under conviction by the message of Stephen, but they resisted, they did anything and everything to stifle that conviction. Not only did they lie, but they got others to lie against this man, who would have laid down his life for any one of them. Stephen was used to heal the sick, perform miracles, and yet they brought false accusations against him. What effect did it have on Stephen?

"And all that sat in the council, looking steadfastly at him, saw his face as it had been the face of an angel."

Something had happened in the life of this man, chosen for menial service, and he became mighty for **God**. How was it accomplished in him? It was because his aim was high; faithful in little, **God** brought him to full fruition. Under the inspiration of divine power by which he spoke, they could not but listen,—even the angels listened, as with holy prophetic utterance he spoke before that council.

Beginning with Abraham and Moses, he continued unfolding the truth. What a marvelous exhortation! Take your Bibles and read it, "listen in" as the angels listened in. As light upon light, truth upon truth, revelation upon revelation, found its way into their calloused hearts, they gazed at him in astonishment; their hearts perhaps became warm at times, and they may have said, "Truly, this man is sent of **God**,"—but when he hurled at them the truth:

"Ye stiffnecked and uncircumcised in heart and ears, ye do always resist the **Holy Ghost**; as your fathers did, so do ye. Which of the prophets have not your fathers persecuted? And they have slain them which showed before of the coming of the Just One; of whom ye have been now the betrayers and murderers; who have received the law by the disposition of angels, and have not kept it."—then what happened? These men were moved; they were "pricked to the heart, and gnashed upon him with their teeth."

There are two marvelous occasions* in the Scriptures where the people were "pricked to the heart." In the second chapter of the Acts of the Apostles, 37th verse, after Peter had delivered that inspired sermon on the Day of Pentecost, the people were "pricked to the heart" with conviction, and there were added to the Church three thousand souls.

Here is Stephen, speaking under the inspiration of the **Holy Ghost**, and the men of this council being "pricked to the heart" rise up as one man to slay him. As you go down through this chapter, from the 55th verse, what a picture you have before you. As I close my eyes, I can get a vision of this scene in every detail—the howling mob with their vengeful, murderous spirit, ready to devour this holy man, and he "being full of the **Holy Ghost**," gazed steadfastly into heaven. What did he see there? From his place of helplessness, he looked up and said:

"Behold, I see the heavens opened, and the Son of Man standing at the right hand of **God**."

Is that the position that **Jesus** went to take? No! He went to "sit" at the right hand of the **Father**; but in behalf of the first martyr, in behalf of the man with that burning flame of **Holy Ghost** power, **God's** Son stood up in honorary testimony of him who, called to serve tables, was faithful unto death. But is that all?

No! I am so glad that it is not all. As the stones came

flying at him, pounding his body, crushing his bones, striking his temple, mangling his beautiful face, what happened? How did this scene end? With that sublime, upward look, this man chosen for an ordinary task but filled with the **Holy Ghost**, was so moved upon by **God** that he finished his earthly work in a blaze of glory, magnifying **God** with his latest breath. Looking up into the face of His Master, he said:"**Lord Jesus**, forgive them! Lay not this sin to their charge!" When he had said this, he fell asleep.

Friends, it is worth dying a thousand deaths to gain that spirit. My **God**! What a divine ending to the life and testimony of a man that was "chosen to serve tables." Without the **Holy Ghost** none of this would have been possible.

CHAPTER SEVEN

We read in Revelation that the testimony of Jesus is the spirit of prophecy.

You will find that true prophetic utterance always exalts the Lamb of God. No prophetic touch is of any good unless there is a FIRE in it. I never expect to be used of God till the FIRE burns.

I feel that if I ever speak, it must be by the Spirit. At the same time remember that the prophet must prophesy according to the measure of faith. If you rise up in your weakness, but rise up in love because you want to honor God, and just begin, you will find the presence of the Lord upon you. Act in faith, and the Lord will meet you.

May God take us on and on into this glorious fact of faith. May we be so in the Holy Ghost that God will work through us on the line of the miraculous and on the lines of prophecy, where we shall always know that it is no longer we but He who is working through us, bringing forth that which is in His divine good pleasure.

WHEN THE FIRE COMES

.Elijah had been mightily used of **God** in calling down **FIRE** and in other miracles, and Elisha is moved with a great spirit of covetousness to have this man's gifts.

You can be very covetous for the gifts of the Spirit, and **God** will allow it. When Elijah said to him, "I want you to stop at Gilgal," Elisha said, **"As the Lord liveth and as thy soul liveth, I will not leave thee."** There was no stopping him. When Elijah wanted Elisha to stop at Jericho, he said in substance, "I am not stopping." The man that stops gets nothing. O, don't stop at Jericho; don't stop at Jordan; don't stop anywhere when **God** would have you move on into all of His fullness that He has for you.

They came to Jordan and Elijah took his mantle and smote the waters. They divided, and Elijah and Elisha went over on the dry ground. Elijah turned to Elisha and said in substance, "Look here, what do you want?"

Elisha was wanting what he was going to have, and you may covet all that **God** says that you shall have. Elisha said**, "I pray thee, let a double portion of thy spirit be upon me."** This was the plow-boy, who had washed the hands of his master; but his spirit got so big that he purposed in his heart that, when Elijah stepped off the scene, he would be put into his place.

Elijah said**, "Thou hast asked a hard thing: nevertheless if thou see me when I am taken from thee, it shall be so unto thee."** May **God** help you never to stop persevering till you get what you want. Let your aspiration be large, and your faith rise until you are wholly on **FIRE** for **God's** best.

Onward they go, and as one steps, the other steps with him. He purposed to keep his eye on his master until the last. It took a chariot of **FIRE** and horses of **FIRE** to part them asunder, and Elijah went up by a whirlwind into heaven. I can fancy I hear Elisha crying out, "**Father** Elijah, drop that mantle!" And it came down. Oh, I can see it lowering, lowering, and lowering.

Elisha took all of his clothes and rent them in two pieces, and then he took up the mantle of Elijah. I do not believe that, when he put on that other mantle, he felt any difference in himself; but when he came to Jordan, he took the mantle of Elijah and smote the waters and said, "Where is the **Lord God** of Elijah?" And the waters parted, and he went over on the dry ground. And the sons of the prophets said, "The spirit of Elijah doth rest upon Elisha."

It is like receiving a gift; you don't know that you have it until you act in faith. Brothers and sisters, as you ask, BELIEVE.

A FLAME OF FIRE

God wants to bring you forth as a flame of **FIRE**, with a message from **God**, with a truth that shall defeat the powers of Satan, with unlimited supply for every needy soul. So, just as John moved the whole of Israel with a mighty cry, you too by the power of the **Holy Ghost** will move the people so that they repent and cry, "What shall we do?"

This is what **Jesus** meant when He said to Nicodemus, "Except a man be born again, he cannot see the kingdom of **God**... that which is born of the flesh is flesh, and that which is born of the Spirit is spirit. Marvel not that I said unto thee, Ye must be born again." If we only knew what these words mean to us, to be born of **God**!

 An infilling of the life of **God**, a new life from **God**, a new creation, living in the world but not of the world, knowing the blessedness of that word, "Sin shall not have dominion over you." How shall we reach this place in the Spirit? By the provision of the **Holy Spirit** that He makes. If we live in the Spirit we shall find all that is carnal swallowed up in life. There is an infilling of the

Spirit which quickens our mortal bodies.

Give **God** your life, and you will see that sickness has to go when **God** comes in fully. Then you are to walk before **God**, and you will find that He will perfect that which concerns you. That is the place where He wants believers to live, the place where the Spirit of the **Lord** comes into your whole being. That is the place of victory.

Look at the disciples. Before they received the **Holy Spirit**, they were in bondage. When Christ said, "One of you shall betray Me," they were all doubtful of themselves and said, "Is it I?" They were conscious of their human depravity and helplessness. Peter said, "Though I should die with Thee, yet will I not deny Thee." The others declared the same, yet they all forsook Him and fled. But after the power of **God** fell upon them in the upper room, they were like lions to meet the difficulty. They were bold. What made them so? The purity and power that is by the Spirit.

God can make you an overcomer. When the Spirit of **God** comes into your surrendered being, He transforms you. There is a life in the Spirit that makes you free, and there is an audacity about it, and there is a personality in it—it is **God** in you.

God can so transform you and change you that all the old order has to go before **God's** new order. Do you think that **God** will make you be a failure? **God** never made man to be a failure. He made man to be a son, to walk the earth in the power of the Spirit, master over the flesh and the devil until nothing arises within him except that which will magnify and glorify the **Lord**.

Jesus came to set us free from sin, to free us from sickness so that we should go forth in the power of the Spirit and minister to the needy, sick and afflicted. Through the revelation of the Word of **God**, we find that divine healing is solely for the glory of **God**, and that salvation is walking in newness of life so that we are inhabited by another, even **God**.

I see people from time to time very slack, cold, and indifferent; but after they get filled with the **Holy Spirit**, they become ablaze for **God**. I believe that **God's** ministers are to be **FLAMES** of **FIRE**; nothing less than **FLAMES**; nothing less than mighty instruments with burning messages.

With a heart full of love, with such a depth of consecration that **God** has taken full charge of the body and it exists only that it may manifest the glory of **God**. Surely, this is the ideal and the purpose of this great plan of salvation for man that we might be filled with all the fullness of **God**, and become ministers of life, **God** working mightily in us and through us to manifest His grace--the saving power of humanity.

"Faith comes by hearing, and hearing by the Word of **God**." It is **God** coming in by His Word and laying the solid foundation. Faith is like dynamite which bursts up the old life and nature by the power of **God** and brings the almighty power of **God** into life.

This substance will diffuse through the whole being, bringing everything else into insignificance. The Word of **God** is formed within the temple. Jeremiah spoke of the Word as a "**FIRE** within." It is a power stronger than granite that can resist the mightiest pressure the devil can bring against it. Faith counts on **God's** coming forth to confound the enemy. Faith count son the display of **God's** might, when it is needful for Him to come forth in power.

UPON THE ALTAR

Brothers, can you be out of **God's** will when you hear His voice? "My sheep hear My voice, and they follow Me." Oh, that **God** today shall help us by the mind of the Spirit to understand. I believe **God** has a message on **FIRE**. He has men clothed by **God**. He has men sent by **God**. Will you be the men? Will you be the women?

You ask, "Can I be the man? Can I be the woman?" Yes, **God** says, "Many are called, but few are chosen." Are you the chosen ones? Those who desire to be chosen, will you allow **God** to choose you? Then He will put His hand upon you. And in the choice He will give you wisdom, He will lead you forth, He will stand by you in the straitened corner, He will lead you every step of the way, for the **Lord**'s anointed shall go forth and bring forth fruit, and their fruit shall remain.

TONGUES AND INTERPRETATION: "Behold, now is

the day of decision. Yield now while the moment of pressure by the presence of **God** comes. Yield now and make your consecration to **God**."

The altar is ready now for all who will obey.

TONGUES AND INTERPRETATION: "The **Lord** is that Spirit that moves in the regenerated, and brings us to the place where **FIRE** can begin and burn, and separate, and transform, and make you all know that **God** has made an inroad into every order. Because we have to be divine, spiritual, changed, and on **FIRE** to catch all the rays of His life, first, burning out; second, transforming; and third, making you fit to live or die."

BAPTISM OF FIRE

But oh, the baptism in the **Holy Ghost**! The baptism of **FIRE**! The baptism of power! The baptism of oneness! The baptism of the association! The baptism of communion! The baptism of the Spirit of life which takes the man shakes him through, builds him up, and makes him know he is a new creature in the Spirit, worshipping **God** in the Spirit.

If my preaching and the preaching of those who come on this platform emphasizes the facts of being baptized with the **Holy Ghost**, and you only have touches of it, if you stop at that, you will be almost as though you were missing the calling. John said by the Spirit:

...He that cometh after me is preferred before me... John 1:15

I indeed baptize you with water unto repentance: but he that cometh after me is mightier than I...he shall baptize you with the **Holy Ghost**, and with **FIRE**. Matthew 3:11

By all means, if you can tarry, you ought to tarry. If you have the Spirit's power upon you, go into that room or somewhere else and never cease till **God** finishes the work. Outside the Pentecostal church where there isn't a revival spirit, and where people are not born again, you will find the church becomes dead, dry, and barren, and helpless. They enter into entertainments and all kinds of teas. They live on a natural association and lose their grand, glorious hope.

WHEN THE FIRE COMES

There are so many wonderful things about a life filled with the **Holy Ghost** that one feels almost as if one were a machine and could never stop speaking of them. There are so many opportunities and such great forces that can never come along any other line. When **Jesus** has come to a place where he will not make bread for himself, [Mt 4.3-4] I find that he reaches a place where he can make bread for thousands. [Mt 14.14-21]

And when I come to a place where I will not do anything for myself, then **God** will do something for me, and I will gladly do anything for him that he may desire me to do. That is in the order of the baptism. It is when we cease to clothe ourselves that **God** clothes us, and it is the clothing wherewith he clothes us that covers all our nakedness.

In his helplessness and brokenness Paul cries: **"Lord, what wilt thou have me to do?" [Ac 9.6]** That cry reached to heaven, and as a result, there came a holy man, touched with the same **FIRE** and zeal that filled his Master, and he laid his hands upon Paul and said, **"Receive thy sight, and be filled with the Holy Ghost." [Ac 9.17]**

[Tongues (by Wigglesworth) and interpretation: "The living touch of the river of the life of **God** is that which makes all things akin, and brings a celestial glory into the human heart, and phrases that meet the kindled desire therein."]

When **God** moves a man his body becomes akin with celestial glory all the time, and the man says things as he is led by the **Holy Ghost** who fills him. When we are filled with the **Holy Ghost** we go forth to see things accomplished that we could never see otherwise. First of all, Paul has a vision. There is always a vision in the baptism of the Spirit. But visions are no good to me except I make them real, except I claim them as they come, except I make them my own; and if your whole desire is to carry out what the Spirit has revealed to you by vision, it will surely come to pass.

Lots of people lack the power because they do not keep

the vision because they do not allow the **FIRE** which has come to infuse into them and continue to burn. There must be a continuous burning on the altar. **Holy Ghost** power in a man is meant to be an increasing force, an enlargement. **God** never has anything of a diminishing type. He is always going on. And I am going on. Are you going on? It is necessary, I tell you, to go on. You must not stop in the plains; [Ge 19.17] there are far greater things for you on the hilltops than in the plains.

Jesus took particular care of Paul; he did not rush him through the business. Some people think that everything ought to be done in a tremendous hurry. With **God**, it is not so. **God** takes plenty of time, and he has a wonderful way of developing things as he goes along. Nothing that you undertake will fail, if only you do not forget what he has told you and if you act upon it.

You really cannot forget that which the **Holy Ghost** brings right into your heart as his purpose for you. A man baptized by the **Holy Ghost** is no longer a natural man; the Spirit forces him; he is turned into another man. Joshua and Caleb could not say anything less than that "**God**, who has taken us and let us see the land; he will surely give us the land." [Nu 13.30]

Where are you fixed? Is **God** the **Holy Ghost** arranging things for you, or are you arranging things according to your plan? A man filled with the **Holy Ghost** has ceased to be, in a sense; he has come to a rest, he has come to where **God** is working, to a place where he can "stand still and see the salvation of the **Lord**." [Ex 14.13] What do I mean? I mean that such a man has ceased from his works and abilities and associations. He will not trust his own heart; he relies only on the omnipotent power of the Most High; he is girded with Another.

The man baptized with the **Holy Ghost** will always keep in touch with his Master in the passing crowd, or wherever he may be. He has no room for anything that steps lower than the unction that was on his Master, or for anything that hinders him from being about his Master's business.

 If you are baptized by the **Holy Ghost**, you have no spiritual food apart from the word of **God**. You have no resources but those that are heavenly; you have been "planted" with Christ, and have "risen with him," [Cl 2.12], and you are "seated with him in heavenly places"; [Ep 2.6] your language is a heavenly language, your source of inspiration is a heavenly touch; **God** is enthroned in your whole life, and you see things "from above," and not from below.

A man that is baptized with the **Holy Ghost** has a **Jesus** mission. He knows his vocation, the plan of his life. **God** speaks to him so definitely and really that there is no mistaking about it. Thank **God** for the knowledge which fixes me so solidly upon **God's** word that I cannot be moved from it by any storm that may rage. The revelation of **Jesus** to my soul by the **Holy Ghost** brings me to a place where I am willing, if need be, to die on what the word says.

The three Hebrew children said, "We are not careful to answer thee in this matter"; [Da 3.16], and when a man of **God** is quickened by the Spirit he never moves toward or depends upon, natural resources. The furnace "one seven times more" heated [Da 3.19] is of no consequence to the men who have heard the voice of **God**; the lions' den has no fearfulness for the man who opens his windows and talks to his **Father**. [Da 6] The people who live in the unction of the Spirit are taken out of the world in the sense that they are kept in the world without being defiled by the evil of the world.

But let us come back to this wonderful vision that Paul had. I want you to see how carefully the **Lord** deals with him. Verse 16: "But rise, and stand upon thy feet: for I have appeared unto thee for this purpose, to make thee a minister and a witness both of these things which thou hast seen, and of those things in the which I will appear unto thee." [Ac 26.16] Do not you see how carefully the **Lord** works? He shows Paul the vision as far as Paul can take it in, and then he says: "There are other things in the which I will again appear unto thee." Did he ever appear unto Paul after that? Certainly, he did. But Paul never lost this vision; he kept it up.

What was there in the vision that held him in such close association with **Jesus** Christ that he was ready for every activity to which the **Holy Ghost** led him? There were certain things he had to do. Look, for instance, at Galatians 1.15-16. There you will find a very wonderful word—a word that has had a great impression upon me about the subject of the continuation of the baptism.

"When it pleased **God**, who separated me from my mother's womb, and called me by his grace, to reveal his Son in me, that I might preach him among the heathen; immediately I conferred not with flesh and blood." [Ga 1.15-16] Now read together with the words: "Therefore I was not disobedient to the heavenly vision," [Ac 26.19] and "I conferred not with flesh and blood."

There is no man here this afternoon who can be clothed in the Spirit, and catch the **FIRE** and zeal of the Master every day and many times in the day, without he ceases in every way to be connected with the "arm of flesh" [2Ch 32.8] which would draw him aside from the power of **God**. Many men have lost the glory because they have been taken up with the natural. If we are going to accomplish in the Spirit the thing **God** has purposed for us, we can never turn again to the flesh. If we are Spirit-filled **God** has cut us short and brought us into a relationship with himself, joined us to Another, and now he is all in all to us.

You may have a vision of the **Lord** all the time you are on a railway train, or in a tramcar, or walking down a street. It is possible to be lonely in the world and to be a Christian, without what? Without you cease to be a natural man. I mean that the Christian ought to have such an unction as to realize at any moment, whether in the presence of others or alone, that he is with **God**. He can have a vision in the tramcar, or the railway train, even if he has to stand with others in front or behind him; or he can have a vision if he is there alone.

Nehemiah stood before the king because of trouble in

Jerusalem which had nigh broken his heart. He was sorrowful, and it affected his countenance; [Ne 2.1-3], but he was so near to **God** that he could say: "I have communed with the **God** of heaven." And if we believers are to go forth and fulfill **God's** purpose with us, the **Holy Spirit** must constantly be filling us and moving upon us until our whole being is on **FIRE** with the presence and power of **God**. That is the order of the baptism of the **Holy Ghost**. The man is then ready for every emergency.

Now it is a most blessed thought struck me as I was reading at our assembly on Sunday morning. That in the holy, radiant glory of the vision that was filling Paul's soul, [Ac 20] the people became so hungry after it that until midnight they drank in at the fountain of his life, and as he was pouring forth a young man fell from the third loft, [Ac 20.9] and Paul, in the same glorious fashion, as always, went down and embraced him and pressed the very life from himself into the young man, and brought him back to life. [Ac 20.10-11]

 Always equipment for emergency, blessed, holy equipment by **God**! Someone calls at your door and wants to see you particularly, but you cannot be seen till you are through with **God**. Living in the **Holy Ghost**, walking in the divine likeness, having no confidence in the flesh, but growing in the grace and knowledge of **God**, and going on from one state of glorious perfection unto another state of perfection—that is it.

You cannot compare the **Holy Ghost** to anything less, but something more, than ever you thought about with all your thoughts. That is the reason why the **Holy Ghost** has to come into us to give us divine revelations for the moment. The man that is a "partaker of the divine nature" [2Pe 1.4] has come into a relationship where **God** imparts his divine mind for the comprehension of his love and the fellowship of his Son. We are only powerful as we know that source, we are only strong as we behold the beatitudes and all the wonderful things and graces of the Spirit.

II

It was a necessity that **Jesus** should live with his disciples for three years, and walk in and out amongst them [Ac 1.21] and manifest his glory, and show it forth day by day. I will show you why it was a necessity. Those men believed in **God**. But this Messiah had continually, day by day, to bring himself into their vision, into their mind, into their very nature. He had to press himself right into their life to make them success after he had ascended to heaven. He had to show them how wonderfully and gracefully and peacefully he could move the crowds.

You remember that the house to which they brought the sick of the palsy, and in which he was speaking to the people, was so crowded that they could not come nigh unto him except by uncovering the roof and dropping the man through. [Mk 2.4] The way to the cities was so pressed with the people [Mk 3.10] who were following **Jesus** and his disciples, which he and they could hardly get along, but he always had time to stop and perform some good deed on the journey thither. What he had to bring home to the minds and hearts of the disciples was that he was truly the Son of **God**.

They never could accomplish what they had to accomplish until he had proved that to them, and until he had soared to the glory. They could only manifest him to others when he had imparted his life into the very core of their nature, and make others confess that they were astonished, and that "we never saw things like this." [Mk 2.12] It was the Son of **God** traveling in the greatness of his strength to manifest before those disciples the keynote of truth that no one could gainsay.

They had been with him and seen his desire, his craving, and his lust to serve **God**. Yes, he lusted to be like **God** in the world manifesting him so that they might see what Philip had missed when **Jesus** said to him, **"Hast thou not seen the Father?" [Jn 14.9]** He wanted them to be clothed with the Spirit, baptized by the Spirit.

Some people get the wrong notion of baptism. The baptism is nothing less than the third person of the blessed trinity coming down from the glory, the executive Spirit of the triune **God** indwelling your body, revealing the truth to you, and causing you sometimes to say "Ah!".

 Our bowels yearn with compassion, as **Jesus** yearned, to travail as he travailed, to mourn as he mourned, to groan as he groaned. It cannot be otherwise with you. You cannot get this thing along a merely passive line. It does not come that way. But, glory is to **God**; it does come. Oh that **God** might bring from our hearts the cry for such a deluge of the Spirit that we could not get away till we were ready for him to fulfill his purpose in us and for us.

I had a wonderful revelation of the power of **God** this last week. If there is anything I know about this baptism it is this: That it is such a force of conviction in my life that I am carried, as it were, through the very depths of it. Sometimes we have to think; at other times we have not time to think, and it is when we are at our wits' end that **God** comes and brings deliverance. When you are at your wits' end, and you throw yourself on the omnipotent power of **God**, what a wonderful transformation there is in a moment.

CHAPTER EIGHT

ALL ON FIRE FOR GOD

There was a young man at the depot that night who had been saved the night before. He was all on **FIRE** to get others saved and purposed in his heart that every day of his life he would get someone saved.

He saw this dejected man and began to speak to him about his soul. He brought him down to our mission and there he came under a mighty conviction of sin. For two and a half hours he was sweating under conviction, and you could see vapor rising from him. At the end of two and a half hours, he was graciously saved.

I said, "**Lord**, tell me what to do." The **Lord** said, "Don't leave him; go home with him." I went to his house. When he saw his wife, he said, "**God** has saved me." The wife broke down, and she too was graciously saved. I tell you there was a difference in that home. Even the cat knew the difference. Previous to this that cat would always run away when that hangs man came into the door. But that night that he was saved the cat jumped on to his knee and went to sleep.

There were two sons in that house, and one of them said to his mother, "Mother, what is up in our house? It was never like this before. It is so peaceful. What is it?" She told him, "**Father** has got saved." The other son was struck with the same thing.

I took this man to many special services, and the power of **God** was on him for many days. He would give his testimony, and as he grew in grace, he desired to preach the gospel. He became an evangelist, and hundreds and hundreds were brought to a saving knowledge of the **Lord Jesus** Christ through his ministry.

TOUCHED BY THE FIRE

When **Jesus** has come to a place where he will not make bread for himself, [Mt 4.3-4] I find that he reaches a place where he can make bread for thousands. [Mt 14.14-21] And when I come to a place where I will not do anything for myself, then **God** will do something for me. I will gladly do anything for him that he may desire me to do. That is in the order of the baptism. It is when we cease to clothe ourselves that **God** clothes us, and it is the clothing wherewith he clothes us that covers all our nakedness.

Smith Wigglesworth When the FIRE Fell

In his helplessness and brokenness Paul cries: "**Lord**, what wilt thou have me to do?" [Ac 9.6] That cry reached to heaven, and as a result, there came a holy man, touched with the same **FIRE** and zeal that filled his Master, and he laid his hands upon Paul and said, "Receive thy sight, and be filled with the **Holy Ghost**." [Ac 9.17]

[Tongues (by Wigglesworth) and interpretation: "The living touch of the river of the life of **God** is that which makes all things akin and brings a celestial glory into the human heart, and phrases that meet the kindled desire therein."]

When **God** moves a man, his body becomes akin with celestial glory all the time, and the man says things as he is led by the **Holy Ghost** who fills him. When we are filled with the **Holy Ghost**, we go forth to see things accomplished that we could never see otherwise. First of all, Paul has a vision.

There is always a vision in the baptism of the Spirit. But visions are no good to me except I make them real, except I claim them as they come, except I make them my own; and if your whole desire is to carry out what the Spirit has revealed to you by vision, it will surely come to pass.

Lots of people lack the power because they do not keep the vision because they do not allow the **FIRE** which has come to infuse into them and continue to burn.

There must be a continuous burning on the altar. **Holy Ghost** power in a man is meant to be an increasing force, an enlargement. **God** never has anything of a diminishing type. He is always going on. And I am going on. Are you going on? It is necessary, I tell you, to go on. You must not stop in the plains; [Ge 19.17] there are far greater things for you on the hilltops than in the plains.

"I conferred not with flesh and blood."

There is no man here this afternoon who can be clothed in the Spirit and catch the **FIRE** and zeal of the Master every day and many times in the day, without he ceases in every way to be connected with the "arm of flesh" [2Ch 32.8] which would draw him aside from the power of **God**.

 Many men have lost the glory because they have been taken up with the natural. If we are going to accomplish in the Spirit the thing **God** has purposed for us, we can never turn again to the flesh. If we are Spirit-filled **God** has cut us short and brought us into a relationship with himself, joined us to another, and now he is all in all to us. You may have a vision of the **Lord** all the time you are on a railway train, or a tramcar, or walking down a street.

It is possible to be lonely in the world and to be a Christian, without what? Without you cease to be a natural man. I mean that the Christian ought to have such an unction as to realize at any moment, whether in the presence of others or alone, that he is with **God**. He can have a vision in the tramcar, or the railway train, even if he has to stand with others in front or behind him; or he can have a vision if he is there alone.

Nehemiah stood before the king because of trouble in Jerusalem which had nigh broken his heart. He was sorrowful, and it affected his countenance; [Ne 2.1-3] but he was so near to **God** that he could say: "I have communed with the **God** of heaven." And if we believers are to go forth and fulfill **God's** purpose with us, the **Holy Spirit** must be constantly filling us and moving upon us until our whole being is on **FIRE** with the presence and power of **God**. That is the order of the baptism of the **Holy Ghost**. The man is then ready for every emergency.

Power from on high

We have a remarkable word in Matthew 3:11, "I indeed baptize you with water unto repentance: but He that cometh after me is mightier than I, whose shoes I am not worthy to bear: He shall baptize you with the **Holy Ghost**, and with **FIRE**." This was the word of one who was filled with the **Holy Ghost** even from his mother's womb, who was so filled with the power of the Spirit of **God** that they came from east and west and from north and south to the banks of the Jordan to hear him.

You have seen water baptism, and you know what it

means. This later baptism taught by this wilderness preacher means that we shall be so immersed, covered and flooded with the blessed **Holy Ghost**, that He fills our whole body.

Now turn to John 7:37-39: "In the last day, that great day of the feast, **Jesus** stood and cried saying, If any man thirst, let him come unto Me, and drink. He that believeth on Me, as the Scripture hath said, out of his belly shall flow rivers of living water. (But this spake He of the Spirit, which they that believe on Him should receive: for the **Holy Ghost** was not yet given; because that **Jesus** was not yet glorified.)"

Jesus saw that the people who had come to the feast, expecting blessing, were going back dissatisfied. He had come to help the needy, to bring satisfaction to the unsatisfied. He does not want any of us to be thirsty, famished, naked, full of discord, full of disorder, full of evil, full of carnality, full of sensuality. And so He sends out in His blessed way the old prophetic cry: "Ho, everyone that thirsteth, come ye to the waters, and he that hath no money; come ye, buy, and eat."

The Master can give you that which will satisfy. He has in Himself just what you need at this hour. He knows your greatest need. You need the blessed **Holy Ghost**, not merely to satisfy your thirst. But to satisfy the needs of thirsty ones everywhere; for as the blessed **Holy Spirit** flows through you like rivers of living water. These floods will break what needs to be broken, they will bring to death that which should be brought to death, but they will bring life and fruitage where there is none.

What do you have? A well of water? That is good as far as it goes. But Christ wants to see a plentiful supply of the river of the **Holy Ghost** flowing through you. Here, on this last day of the feast, we find Him preparing them for the Pentecostal fullness that was to come, the fullness that He should shed forth from the glory after His ascension.

Note the condition necessary—"He that believeth on Me" This is the root of the matter. Believe on Him. Believing on Him will bring forth this river of blessedness. Abraham believed **God**, and we are all blessed through faithful Abraham. As we believe **God**, many will be blessed through our faith. Abraham was an extraordinary man of faith. He believed **God** in the face of everything. **God** wants to bring us to the place of believing, where, despite all contradictions around, we are strong in faith, giving **God** glory. As we fully believe **God**, He will be glorified, and we will prove a blessing to the whole world as was our **Father**, Abraham.

Turn to John 14. Here we see the promise that ignorant and unlearned fishermen were to be clothed with the Spirit, anointed with power from on high, and endued with the Spirit of wisdom and knowledge. He imparts divine wisdom; you will not act foolishly. The Spirit of **God** will give you a sound mind, and He will impart to you the divine nature.

How could these weak and helpless fishermen, poor and needy, ignorant and unlearned, do the works of Christ and greater works than He had done? They were incapable. None of us is able. But our emptiness has to be clothed with divine fullness, and our helplessness has to be filled with the power of His helpfulness. Paul knew this when he gloried in all that brought him down in weakness, for flowing into his weakness came a mighty deluge of divine power.

Christ knew that His going away would leave His disciples like a family of orphans. But He told them it was expedient, it was best, for after His return to the **Father** He would send the Comforter, and He would come to indwell them. "Ye in Me, and I in you."

Christ said, "And I will pray for the **Father**, and He shall send you another Comforter, that He may abide with you forever; even the Spirit of truth." What a fitting name for the One who was coming to them at the time they were bereft—Comforter. After Christ had left them, there was a great need, but that need was met on the day of Pentecost when the Comforter came.

You will always find that in the moment of need the **Holy Spirit** is a comforter. When my dear wife was lying dead, the doctors could do nothing. They said to me, "She's gone; we cannot help you." My heart was so moved that I said, "O **God**, I cannot spare her!" I went up to her and said, "Oh, come back, come back, and speak to me! Come back; come back!" The Spirit of the **Lord** moved, and she came back and smiled again. But then the **Holy Ghost** said to me, "She's mine. Her work is done. She is mine."

Oh, that comforting word! No one else could have

spoken it. The Comforter came. From that moment my dear wife passed out. And on this day the Comforter has a word for every bereaved one.

Christ further said, "But the Comforter, which is the **Holy Ghost**, whom the **Father** will send in My name, He shall teach you all things, and bring all things to your remembrance, whatsoever I have said unto you." How true this is. From time to time He takes of the words of Christ and makes them life to us. And, empowered with this blessed Comforter, the words that we spake under the anointing are spirit and life.

There are some who come to our meetings which, when you ask them whether they are seekers, reply, "Oh, I am ready for anything." I tell them, "You will never get anything." It's necessary to have the purpose that the Psalmist had when he said, "One thing have I desired of the **Lord**, that will I seek after." When the **Lord** reveals to you that you must be filled with the **Holy Ghost**, seek that one thing until **God** gives you that gift.

I spoke to two young men in a meeting one day. They were preachers. They had received their degrees. I said to them, "Young men, what about it?"

"Oh," they said, "we do not believe in receiving the **Holy Ghost** in the same way as you people do."

I said to them, "You are dressed up like preachers, and it is a pity having to have the dress without the Presence."

"Well, we do not believe it the way you do," they said.

"But look," I said, "the apostles believed it that way. Wouldn't you like to be like the apostles? You have read how they received at the beginning, haven't you?"

Always remember this, that the Baptism will always be as at the beginning. It has not changed. If you want a real Baptism, expect it just the same way as they had it at the beginning.

These preachers asked, "What had they at the beginning?"

I quoted from the tenth chapter of Acts where it says, "On the Gentiles also was poured out the gift of the **Holy Ghost**. For they heard them speak with tongues and magnify **God**." The Jews knew that these Gentiles had the same kind of experience as they had at the beginning on the day of Pentecost. The experience has not changed; it is still the same as at the beginning.

When these two young men realized that Peter and John and the rest of the disciples had received the mighty endowment at the beginning and that it was for them, they walked up to the front where folk was tarrying. They were finely dressed, but in about half an hour they looked different.

They had been prostrated. I had not caused them to do it. But they had been so lost and so controlled by the power of **God**, and were so filled with the glory of **God**, that they just rolled over, and their fine clothes were soiled, but their faces were radiant. What caused the change?

They had received what the hundred and twenty received at the beginning.

These young preachers had been ordained by men. Now they received an ordination that was better. The **Lord** had ordained them that they should go and bring forth much fruit. The person that receives this ordination goes forth with fresh feet—his feet shod with the preparation of the gospel of peace; he goes forth with a fresh voice— it speaks as the Spirit gives utterance; he goes forth with a fresh mind—a mind illuminated by the power of **God**; he goes forth with a fresh vision and sees all things new.

When I was in Switzerland, a woman came to me and said, "Now that I am healed and have been delivered from that terrible carnal oppression that bound and fettered me, I feel that I have a new mind. I should like to receive the **Holy Ghost**; but when I hear these people at the altar making so much noise, I feel like running away."

Shortly after this, we were in another place in Switzerland where there was a great hotel joined to the building where we were ministering. At the close of one of the morning services, the power of **God** fell. That is the only way I can describe it—the power of **God** fell. This poor, timid creature, who could not bear to hear any noise, screamed so loud that all the waiters in this big hotel came out, with their aprons on and their trays, to see what was up. Nothing especially was "up," something had come down, and it so altered the situation that this woman could stand anything after that.

When you receive the Baptism, remember the words in 1 John 2:20, "Ye have an unction from the Holy One." **God** grant that we may not forget that. Many people, instead of standing on the rock of faith to believe that they have received this unction, say, "Oh, if I could only feel the unction!"

Brother, your feeling robs you of your greatest unction. Your feelings are often on the line of discouragement. You have to get away from the walk by sense, for **God** has said, "The just shall live by his faith." Believe what **God** says, "Ye have an unction from the Holy One," an unction from above. All thoughts of holiness, all thoughts of purity, all thoughts of power are from above.

Frequently I see a condition of emergency. Here is a woman, dying; here is a man who has lost all the powers of his faculties; here is a person apparently in death. **God** does not want me to be filled with anxiety. What does He want me to do? To believe only. After you have received, only believe. Dare to believe the One who has declared, "I will do it."

Christ says, "Verily I say unto you, That whosoever shall say unto this mountain, Be thou removed, and be thou cast into the sea; and shall not doubt in his heart, but shall believe that those things which he saith shall come to pass; he shall have whatsoever he saith." **God** declares, "Ye have an unction." Believe **God**, and you will see this happen. What you say will come to pass. Speak the word, and the bound shall be free, the sick shall be healed. "He shall have whatsoever he saith." "Ye have an unction." The unction has come, the unction abides, the unction is with us.

But what about it, if you have not lived in the place where the unction can be increased? What is the matter? There is something between you and the Holy One— some uncleanness, some impurity, some desire that is not of Him; something that has come in the way? Then the Spirit is grieved. Has the unction left? No. When He comes in, He comes to abide. Make confession of your sin, of your failure, and once more the precious blood of **Jesus** Christ will cleanse, and the grieved Spirit will once more manifest Himself.

John further says, "The anointing which ye have received of Him abideth in you." We have an anointing, the same anointing which **Jesus** Christ Himself received. For "**God** anointed **Jesus** of Nazareth with the **Holy Ghost** and with power; who went about doing good." The same anointing is for us.

It means much to have a continuous faith for tho manifestation of the anointing. At the death of Lazarus, when it seemed that Mary and Martha and all around them had lost faith, **Jesus** turned to the **Father** and said, "**Father**, I thank Thee that Thou hast heard Me. And I knew that Thou hearest Me always." Before that supreme faith that counted on **God**, that counted on His anointing, death had to give up Lazarus.

Through a constant fellowship with the **Father**, through bold faith in the Son, through a mighty unction of the blessed **Holy Spirit**, there will come a right of way for **God** to be enthroned in our hearts, purifying us so thoroughly that there is no room for anything but the divine Presence within. And through the manifestation of this Presence, the works of Christ and greater works shall be accomplished for the glory of our Triune **God!**.

CHAPTER NINE

A liquid, holy, indispensable, real FIRE in my bosom

When the Man of Sin comes, he will be hailed 'on all sides. When he is manifested, who will miss him? Why the reverent, the holy the separated. How will they miss him? Because they will not be here to greet him!

But there will be things that will happen before his coming that we shall know. You can tell. I am like one this morning that is moving with a liquid, holy, indispensable, real **FIRE** in my bosom, and I know it is burning, and the body is not consumed. It is real **FIRE** from heaven that is making my utterances come to you to know that He is coming. He is on the way **God** is going to help me tell you why you will know. You that have the breath of the Spirit, there is something now moving as I speak As I speak, this breath of mighty, quickening, moving, changing, desirable power is making you know, and it is this alone that is making you know that you will be ready.

No matter who misses it, you will be ready. It is this I want to press upon you this morning, that you will be ready. And you won't question your position. You will know. Ah! Thank **God**, ye are not of the night. Ye are of the day. It shall not overtake you as a thief. Ye are the children of the day.

You are not the night. You are not drunken. Yes, you are. There is so much intoxication from this holy incarnation that makes you feel all the time you have to have Him hold you up. Praise the **Lord**! Holy intoxication, inspired revelation, invocation, incessantly inwardly moving your very nature, that you know as sure as anything that you do not belong to those who are putting off the day. You are hastening unto the day you are longing for the day.

You say "What a great day!" Why do you say it? Because the creature — Is this body the creature? No. This is the temple that holds the creature. The creature inside the temple longeth, travaileth, groaneth to be delivered, and will be delivered. It is the living creature. It is a new creature. It' is the new creation. It is a new nature. It is a new life.

What manner of men ought we to be? I am going to read it:

The **Lord** is not slack concerning his promise, as some men count slackness; but is longsuffering to us-ward, not willing that any should perish, but that all should come to repentance —2 Peter 3:9.

I want you to notice this: This is not the wicked repentant. The epistles are always speaking to the saints of **God**. When I speak to you saints of **God**, you will find that my language will make you see that there is not within you one thing that has to be covered. I say it without fear of contradiction because it is my whole life, inspired by the truth. You know that these meetings will purify you.

It is on this line that every time you hear people speak upon this — I do not mean as a theory. This is not a theory. There is a difference between a man standing before you on theory. He has chapter and verse, line upon line, precept upon precept, and he works it. Out upon the scriptural basis.

It is wonderful, it is good, it is inspiring, but I am not there this morning. Mine is another touch. Mine is the spiritual nature showing to you that the world is ripening for judgment. Mine is a spiritual acquaintance bringing you to a place of separation, holiness unto **God**, that you may purify yourself and be clean, ready for the great day.

This is the day of purifying. This is the day of holiness. This is the day of separation. This is the day of waking. O **God**, let us wake today! Let the inner spirit wake into consciousness that **God** is calling us. The **Lord** is upon us. We see that the day is upon us. We look at the left side; we look at the right side, we see everywhere new theories. New things will not stand the light of the truth. When you see these, things; you know that there must be a great falling away before the day And it is coming. It is upon us.

Paul said he travailed in birth. **Jesus** did the same. John had the same. So brothers and sisters, may **God** bless you and make you see that this is a day of travailing for the Church of **God** that she might be formed so that she is ready for putting on the glorious raiment of heaven forever and forever.

Seeing then that all these things shall be dissolved, what manner of persons ought ye to be in all holy conversation and godliness, Looking for and hasting unto the coming of the day of **God**, wherein the heavens being on **FIRE** shall be dissolved, and the elements shall melt with fervent heat?

Nevertheless we, according to his promise, look for new heavens and a new earth, wherein dwelleth righteousness. Wherefore, beloved, seeing that ye look for such things, be diligent that ye may be found of him in peace, without spot, and blameless —2 Peter 3:11-14.

Without spot! WITHOUT SPOT! Without spot and blameless!

Do you believe it? Who can do it? THE BLOOD CAN DO IT! The blood, the blood, oh the blood! The blood of the Lamb! The blood of **Jesus** can do it. Spotless, clean, preserved for **God**.

RECEIVE THE FIRE FROM GOD

There is life through the power of it, and as we receive the Word in faith, we receive the nature of **God** Himself. It is as we lay hold of **God's** promises in simple faith that we become partakers of the divine nature. As we receive the Word of **God**, we come right into touch with a living force, a power which changes nature into grace, a power that makes dead things live, a power which is of **God**, which will be manifested in our flesh.

This power has come forth with its glory to transform us by divine act into sons of **God**, to make us like unto THE Son of **God**, by the Spirit of **God** who moves us on from grace to grace and from glory to glory as our faith rests in this living Word.

It is important that we have a foundation truth, something greater than ourselves, on which to rest. In Hebrews 12 we read, "Looking unto **Jesus**, the author, and finisher of our faith." **Jesus** is our life, and He is the power of our life. We see in the 5th chapter of Acts that as soon as Peter was let out of prison the word of **God** came, "Go speak... all the words of this life." There is only one Book that has life. In this Word, we find Him who came that we might have life and have it more abundantly, and by faith, this life is imparted to us.

When we come into this life by divine faith (and we must realize that it is by grace we are saved through faith and that it is not of ourselves, but is the gift of **God**), we become partakers of this life. This Word is greater than anything else. There is no darkness at all in it.

Anyone who dwells in this Word is able under all circumstances to say that he is willing to come to the light that his deeds may be made manifest. But outside of this Word is darkness, and the manifestations of darkness will never come to light because their deeds are evil. But the moment we are saved by the power of the Word of **God** we love the light, the truth. The inexpressible divine power, force, passion, and **FIRE** that we receive is of **God**. Drink, my beloved, drink deeply of this Source of life.

Faith is the substance of things hoped for. Someone said to me one day, "I would not believe in anything I could not handle and see," Everything you can handle and see is temporary and will perish with the using. But the things not seen are eternal and will not fade away.

Are you dealing with tangible things or with the eternal things, the things that are facts that are made real to faith? Thank **God** that through the knowledge of the truth of the Son of **God** I have within me a greater power, a mightier working, an inward impact of life, of power, of vision and of truth more real than anyone can know who lives in the realm of the tangible. **God** manifests Himself to the person who dares to believe.

But there is something more beautiful than that. As we receive divine life in the new birth, we receive a nature that delights in doing the will of **God**. As we believe the Word of **God** a well of water springs up within our heart.

Spring is always better than a pump. But I know that a spring is apt to be outclassed when we get the Baptism of the **Holy Ghost**.

FLAMES OF FIRE

I was going into a big meeting in London one day, and a man who stood in the doorway said to me, "Don't you know me?" I said, "No, I do not recognize you just at this moment." "Don't you know my daughter?" he said. "No." "Nor my wife?" They all stood there. "No, I seem to have lost recollection of you." "Well," he said, "I am Smith from Brighton." Then I recognized them.

"Now," he said, "look at her," turning to his daughter, a beautiful young woman. They brought her to me stretched out in a carriage where she had been for years and years, helpless; had to be lifted about, and in a moment, as soon as **God's** touch came upon her, from the crown of her head to the sole of her foot, [Is 1.6] there wasn't a weakness. She was perfect and had been walking ever since. No man can do those things. There has never been a man living who could do it; only the man Christ **Jesus**, and if we wish to be used in that way we shall have to have him, know him, and understand him, for he is the Holy One.

The ministry of healing became so mighty in Australia that in some places I had to give up a day to minister to the sick, beginning at 9 and continuing until 4 o'clock to get through, praying with nearly 700 people. There is a chance for a lifetime.

You talk about opportunity; I would not take the world's worth for the opportunity, and we ought to buy up our opportunities. You never will know what you have until you experiment upon what you have in faith. Every man that has ever done anything for **God** was amazed to find **God** respond the first time he ventured out in faith.

I say all these things to you to move you into a living faith in **God**; for what will it profit me without some of you are turned into **FLAMES** of **FIRE**? What will it profit me if I turn from these meetings and you have only heard my voice and seen me? **God** would never have John and Peter and James to move up and down the world and leave people where they found them.

They were to make disciples of all nations, [Mt 28.19] and in the name of **Jesus** I am here, as it were, to make disciples; to create within you a deeper thirst and a longing for deeper things of **God**. If this is not my object, I ought not to be here. We have a higher calling, a nobler calling than to be fascinated with things of ourselves. It is not the fascination of ourselves; it is the inward **FIRE** that burns by the power of **God**, that attracts.

CATH THE FIRE

If you turn to the seventh chapter of the Acts of the Apostles and
read the prophecy that Stephen utters, it is most sublime.

Smith Wigglesworth When the FIRE Fell

As he prophesied under the power of the Spirit, the power of the devil came upon those people; they couldn't stand it. It meant his death, but it was in the power of the Spirit. There is something about the prophecy that makes you know it is **God**.

Here is a man in the assembly who starts in to pray. He has prayed many times in the assembly, and you have been blessed, but suddenly you catch **FIRE**, and you feel the inspiration as the Spirit prays through him, and you know when **God** has finished and when he begins his prayer. The lesson to learn in Pentecost is when to finish, for it is a serious thing to go on after the **Lord** has finished. You begin in the Spirit and end in the flesh. The same thing is true of prophecy; they begin in the Spirit and end in the flesh.

Then there are some foolish people in the world who, when they know someone has the gift of prophecy, go around to his house and try to find out something by prophecy. That is as bad as going to a medium. Do you think you can get a prophetic message on those lines? Now listen: Wisdom is justified by her children, [Lk 7.35] and if you do not keep in wisdom, nobody wants anything to do with you, so do not work along those lines. If you want to know the mind of **God**, get it in the book; you do not need a prophet to tell you. **God** is his interpreter.

I was saved when I was a boy eight years old, and I have never lost the witness. I never went to school, and so I had no chance to learn to read. When I got married, my wife taught me both to read and write, though she could never teach me to spell, I do the best I can. I so love the word of **God**. I do not remember spending any time but with the word. Papers and books have no fascination for me. The word of **God** is my meat and my drink. I get a fresh breath from heaven every time I read it. It is full of prophetic utterances that make my soul rejoice.

TONGUES AND INTERPRETATION:

"**God** confirms in us faith that we may be refined in the world, having neither spot nor blemish nor any such thing. It is all on the line of faith, he that hath faith overcomes – it is the **Lord** Who purifies and bringeth where the **FIRE** burns up all the dross, and anoints with fresh oil; see to it that ye keep pure. **God** is separating us for Himself.

"…I will give you a mouth and wisdom, which all your adversaries will not be able to gainsay nor resist" (Luke 21:15). The **Holy Spirit** will tell you at the moment what you shall say. The world will not understand you, and you will find as you go on with **God** that you do not under-stand fully. We cannot comprehend what we are saved to, or from. None can express the joy of **God's** indwelling. The **Holy Spirit** can say through you the need of the moment. The world knows us not because it knew Him not.

"Who is he that overcomes the world, but he that believes **Jesus** is the Son of **God**?" (1 John 5:5). A place of confidence in **God**, a place of prayer, a place of knowledge, that we have what we ask because we keep His commandments and do the things that are pleasing in His sight. Enoch before his translation had the testimony; he had been well-pleasing unto **God**. We overcome by believing.

Message Red-Hot, Burning, and Living.

For if the ministration of condemnation is glory, much more doth the ministration of righteousness exceed in glory. 2 Corinthians 3:6-9

Let us enter into these great words on the line of holy thoughtfulness. If I go on with **God**, He wants me to understand all His deep things. He doesn't want anybody in the Pentecostal church to be novices, or to deal with the Word of **God** on natural grounds. We can understand the Word of **God** only by the Spirit of **God**.

We cannot define, or separate, or deeply investigate and unfold this holy plan of **God** without we have the life of **God**, the thought of **God**, the Spirit of **God**, and the revelation of **God**. The Word of Truth is pure, spiritual, and divine. If you try to divide it on natural grounds, you will only finish up on natural lines for natural man, but you will never satisfy a Pentecostal Assembly.

The spiritual people can only be fed on spiritual material. So if you are expecting your messages to catch **FIRE**, you will have to have them on **FIRE**. You won't have to light the message up in the meeting. You will have to bring the message red-hot, burning, and living.

The message must be direct from heaven. It must be as truly, "Thus saith the **Lord**," as the Scriptures which are, "Thus saith the **Lord**," because you will only speak as the Spirit gives utterance, and you will always be giving fresh revelation. You will never be stale on any line, whatever you will be fruitful, elevating the mind, lifting the people, and all the people will want more.

To come into this, we must see that we not only need the baptism of the Spirit, but we need to come to a place where there is only the baptism of the Spirit left. Look at the first verse of the fourth chapter of Luke, and you will catch this beautiful truth:

And **Jesus** being full of the **Holy Ghost** returned from Jordan and was led by the Spirit into the wilderness.

But look at Mark 1: 12 and you will find He was driven of the Spirit into the wilderness:

And immediately the Spirit driveth him into the wilderness.

In John's gospel **Jesus** says He does not speak or act of Himself:

…the words that I speak unto you I speak not of myself: but tbe Father that dwelleth in me, he doeth the works. John 14:10

We must know that the baptism of the Spirit immerses us

into an intensity of zeal, into a likeness to **Jesus**, to make us into pure, running metal so hot for **God** that it travels like oil from vessel to vessel. This divine line of the Spirit will let us see that we have ceased and we have begun. We are at the end for a beginning. We are down and out, and **God** is in and out.

There isn't a thing in the world that can help us in this meeting. There isn't a natural thought that can be of any use here. There isn't a thing that is carnal, earthly, natural, that can ever live in these meetings. It must only have one pronouncement; it has to die eternally because there is no other plan for a baptized soul, only dead indeed.

God, help us to see then that we may be filled with the letter without being filled with the Spirit. We may be filled with knowledge without having divine knowledge. And we may be filled with wonderful things on natural lines and remain a natural man. But you cannot do it in this truth that I am dealing with this morning.

No man can walk this way without He is in the Spirit. He must live in the Spirit, and he must realize all the time that he is growing in that same ideal of his Master, in season and out of season, always beholding the face of the Master, **Jesus**. David says, "I foresaw the **Lord** for He was on my right hand that I should not be moved. Then my tongue was glad." Praise the **Lord**!

For even that which was made glorious had no glory in this respect, because of the glory that excelleth. For if that which is done away was glorious, much more that which remaineth is glorious. 2 Corinthians

3:10,11

I notice here that the one has to be done away, and the other has to increase. One day I was having a good time on this chapter. I had a lot of people before me who were living on the 39 Articles and Infant Baptism, and all kinds of things. The **Lord** showed me that all these things had to be done away. I find there is no place into all the further plan with **God** without you putting them to one side. "Done away."

Is it possible to do away with the commandments? Yes and no. If they are not so done away with you that you have no consciousness of keeping commandments, then they are not done away. If you know you are living holy, you don't know what holiness is. If you know you are keeping commandments, you don't know what keeping commandments are.

These things are done away. **God** has brought us in to be holy without knowing it, and keeping the whole truth without knowing it, living in it, moving in it, acting in it, a new creation in the Spirit. The old things are done away. If there is any trouble with you at all, it shows you have not come to the place where you are at rest.

"Done away." **God**, help us to see it. If the teaching is a bit too high for you, ask the **Lord** to open your eyes to come into it. For there is no man here has power in prayer or has power in life with **God** if he is trying to keep the commandments.

They are done away, brother. And thank **God**, the very doing away with them is fixing them deeper in our hearts than ever before. For out of the depths we cry unto **God**, and in the depths has He turned righteousness in, and uncleanness out. It is unto the depths we cry unto **God** in these things. May **God** lead us all every step of the way in His divine leading.

How does Satan get an opening into a believer's life?

When the saint ceases to seek after holiness, purity, righteousness, truth; when he ceases to pray, stops reading the Word and gives way to carnal appetites, then it is that Satan comes.

So often sickness comes as a result of disobedience. David said, "Before I was afflicted, I went astray." Seek the **Lord** and He will sanctify every thought, every act, till your whole being is ablaze with holy purity and your one desire will be for Him who has created you in holiness. Oh, this holiness!

Can we be made pure? We can. Every inbred sin must go. **God** can cleanse away every evil thought. Can we have a hatred for sin and a love for righteousness? Yes, **God** will create within thee a pure heart. He will take away the stony heart out of the flesh. He will sprinkle thee with clean water and thou shalt be cleansed from all thy filthiness. When will He do it? When you seek Him for such inward purity, it will come.

* **This is the day of purifying**.

This is the day of holiness. This is the day of separation. This is the day of waking. O **God**, let us wake today! Let the inner spirit wake into consciousness that **God** is calling us. The **Lord** is upon us. We see that the day is upon us. We look at the left side, we look at the right side, we see everywhere new theories. New things will not stand the light of the truth When you see these, things, you know that there must be a great falling away before the day and it is coming. It is upon us."

CHAPTER TEN

SMITH WIGGLESWORTH

A Straightened Place

Gen 32:24: And Jacob was left alone, and there wrestled a man with him until the breaking of the day. As we look back over our spiritual career, we shall always see there has been a good deal of our day, and that the end of our day was the beginning of **God** day. Can two walk together, except they are agreed?

Flesh and blood cannot inherit the kingdom of **God**, neither doth corruption inherit incorruption, and we cannot enter the deep things of **God** until we are free from our ideas and ways. Jacob! The name means supplanter, and when Jacob came to the end of his way **God** had a way.

How slow we are to see that there is a better day.

Beloved, the glory is never as wonderful as when **God** has His plan, and we are helpless and throw down our sword and give up our authority to another. Jacob was a great worker, and he would go through any hardship if he could have his way.

In many ways, he had his way, and in ignorance how gloriously **God** preserved him from calamity. There is a good, and there is a better, but **God** has a best, a higher standard for us than we have yet attained. It is a better thing if it is **God's** plan and not ours.

Jacob and his mother had a plan to secure the birthright and the blessing, and his **Father** agreed to his going to Padan-aram, but **God** planned the ladder and the angels. The land whereon thou liest, to thee, will I give it I am with thee and will keep thee in all places whither thou goest, and will bring thee again into this land; for I will not leave thee until I have done that which I have spoken to thee of.

What a good thing for the lad, amid the changes, **God** obtained the right place. The planning for the birthright had not been a nice thing, but here at Bethel, he found **God** was with him. Many things may happen in our lives, but when the veil is lifted, and we see the glory of **God**, His tender compassion over us all the time, to be where **God** is, how wonderful it is.

Bethel was the place where the ladder was set up twenty-one years before. Twenty-one years of wandering and fighting and struggling. Listen to his conversation with his wives: Your **Father** hath deceived me and changed my wages ten times, but **God** suffered him not to hurt me. To his **Father**-in-law: Except the **God** of my **Father** had been with me, thou hadst sent me away empty. **God** hath seen my affliction and the labor of my hands.

Jacob had been out in the bitter frost at night watching the flocks. He was a thrifty man, a worker, a planner, a supplanter. We see the whole thing around us in the world today "supplanters. There may be a measure of blessing, but **God** is not first in their lives. We are out judging them, but there is a better way, better than our best. **God's** way. **God** first! There is a way that seemeth right unto a man, but the end thereof are the ways of death.

But there is a way that **God** establishes, and I want us to keep that way before us this morning" the way that **God** establishes. In our natural planning and way, we may have many blessings, of a kind; but oh, beloved, the trials the hardships, the barrenness, the things missed which **God** could not give us! I realize this morning by the **Holy Ghost**; I realize by the anointing of the **Spirit** that there is a freshness, a glow, planning in **God** where you can know that **God** is with you all the time. Can we know that **God** is with us all the time? Yes! Yes! Yes! I tell you there is a place to reach where all that **God** has for us can flow through us to a needy world all the time.

For as the heavens are higher than the earth, so are My ways higher than your ways, and My thoughts than your thoughts. Verse 24: And Jacob was left alone, and there wrestled a man with him until the breaking of the day. Oh, to be left alone! Alone with **God**! In the context, we read that several things had gone on. His wives had gone on, his children had gone on, and all had gone on. His sheep and oxen had gone on, his camels and asses had gone on, all had gone on. He was alone.

You will often find you are alone. Whether you like it or not, your wives will go on; your children will go on, your cattle will go on. Jacob was left alone. His wife could not make atonement for him, his children could not make atonement for him, and his money was useless to help him. And Jacob was left alone, and there wrestled a man with him until the breaking of the day.

What made Jacob come to that place of loneliness, weakness, and knowledge of himself? The memory of the grace with which **God** had met him **twenty-one years before**, when he saw the ladder and the angels. He had heard the voice of **God**: Behold I am with thee and will keep thee, and will bring thee again into this land; for I will not leave thee until I have done that which I have spoken to thee of.

He remembered Gods mercy and grace. Here he was returning to meet Esau. His brother had become very rich, he was a chief, he had been blessed abundantly in the things of this world, and he had authority and power to bind all Jacob had and to take vengeance upon him. Jacob knew this. He also knew that there was only one way of deliverance.

What was it? The mind of **God**. No one can deliver me but **God**. **God** had met him twenty-one years before when he went out to empty. He had come back with wives and children and goods, but he was lean in soul and impoverished in **Spirit**. Jacob said to himself, If I do not get a blessing from **God,** I can never meet Esau, and he made up his mind he would not go on until he knew that he had favor with **God**.

Jacob was left alone, and unless we get alone with **God**, we shall surely perish. **God** interposes where strife is at an end; the way of revelation is plain, and the **Holy Ghost**s plan is so clear, that we have to say it was **God** after all Jacob was left alone. He knelt alone. The picture is so real to me.

Alone! Alone! Alone! He began to think. He thought about the ladder and the angels. I think as he began to pray his tongue would cleave to the roof of his straitened place, which revealed the face of **God's** mouth.

Jacob had to get rid of a lot of things. It had all been Jacob! Jacob! Jacob! He got alone with **God**, and he knew it if you get alone with **God**, what a place of revelation! Alone with **God**! Jacob was left alone, alone with **God**. We stay too long with our relations, our camels and our sheep. Jacob was left alone. It would be an afternoon.

So hour after hour passed. He began to feel the presence of **God**. But **God** was getting disappointed with Jacob. If ever **God** is disappointed with you when you tarry in his presence, it will be because you are not white-hot. If you do not get hotter, and hotter, and hotter, you disappoint **God**. If **God** is with you and you know it, be in earnest.

Pray! Pray! Pray! Lay hold! Hold fast the confidence and the rejoicing of the hope firm unto the end. If you do not, you disappoint **God**. Jacob was that way. **God** said: you are not real enough; you are not hot enough; you are too ordinary; you are no good to me unless you are filled with zeal, white hot!

He said, Let me go, for the day breaketh. Jacob knew if **God** went without blessing him, Esau could not be met. If you are left alone with **God** and you cannot get to a place of victory, it is a terrible time. You must never let go, whenever you are seeking â fresh revelation, light on the path, some particular need, never let go.

Victory is ours if we are in earnest enough. All must pass on, nothing less will please **God**. Let me go, the day breaketh! He was wrestling with equal strength. Nothing is obtained that way. You must always master that which you are wrestling with. If darkness covers you if it is the fresh revelation you need, or your mind to be relieved, always get the victory.

 God says you are not in earnest enough. Oh, you say, the Word does not say that. But it was Gods mind. In wrestling, the strength is in the neck, chest, and thigh; the thigh is the strength of all. So, **God** touched his thigh. That strength is gone, defeat is sure.

 What did Jacob do? He hung on. **God** means to have a people severed by the power of His power, so hold fast; He will never leave go. And if we do leave go, we shall fall short. Jacob said I will not let Thee go, except Thou bless me. And **God** blessed him.

 Verse 28: Thy name shall be called no more Jacob, but Israel. Now a new order is beginning, sons of **God**. How wonderful the change of Jacob to Israel! Israel! Victory all the time, **God** building all the time, **God** enough all the time. Power over Esau, power over the world, and power over the cattle.

The cattle are nothing to him now. All are in subjection as he comes out of the great night of trial. The sun rises upon him. Oh, that **God** may take us on, the sun rising, **God** supplanting all! What after that?

Read how **God** blessed and honored him. Esau meets him. No fighting now. What a blessed state of grace! They kissed each other. When a man's ways please the **Lord**, he maketh his enemies to be at peace with him. What about all these cattle, Jacob? Oh, its a present.

Oh, I have plenty; I dont want your cattle. What a joy it is to see your face again! What a wonderful change! Who wrought it? **God**. Verse 25: When he saw that he prevailed not against Him. Could he hold **God**? Can you hold **God**? It is irreverent to say oh, yes, you can. Sincerity can hold Him, dependence can hold Him, and weakness can hold Him.

When you are weak, then are you strong. I tell you what cannot hold Him. Self-righteousness cannot hold Him; pride cannot hold Him, the assumption cannot hold Him, high-mindedness cannot hold Him; thinking you are something when you are nothing, puffed up in your imagination.

Nothing but sincerity! You can hold Him in the closet, in the prayer meeting, everywhere. If any man hears my voice and open the door I will come in and will sup with him, and he with me. Can you hold Him? There may be a thought, sometimes, that He has left you. Oh, no! He does not leave Jacob, Israel. What changed his name? The wrestling?

What changed his name? The holding on, the clinging, the brokenness of **Spirit**? If you do not help me I am no good, no good for the worlds needs. I am no longer salt. Jacob obtained the blessing on two lines: the favor of **God**, and a yieldedness of will. Gods **Spirit** was working in him to bring him to a place of helplessness; **God** co-working to bring him to Bethel, the place of victory.

Jacob remembered Bethel, and through all the mischievous conditions he had kept his vow. When we make vows and keep them, how **God** helps us, we must call upon **God** and give Him an account of the promise.

Verse 30: And Jacob called the name of the place Peniel, for I have seen **God** face to face, and my life is preserved. How did he know? Do you know when **God** blesseth you when you have victory? But twenty years afterwards the **VISION** of the ladder and the angels! How did he know?

We must have a perfect knowledge of what **God** has for us. He knew that he had the favor of **God** and that no man could hurt him. Let us in all our seeking see we have the favor of **God**, walking day by day beneath open heaven.

Keeping His commandments, walking in the **Spirit**, tender in our hearts, lovable, appreciated by **God**; if so, we shall be appreciated by others, and our ministry will be a blessing to those who hear. **God** bless you. **God** bless you for **Jesus** sake.

Pentecostal power, The

Bible Reading Acts 19:1-20.

This is a wonderful reading; it has many things in it which indicate to us that there was something more marvelous about it than human power, and when I think about Pentecost I am astonished from day to day because of its mightiness, of its wonderfulness and how the glory overshadows it. I sometimes think about these things, and they make me feel we have only just touched it. Truly it is so, but we must thank **God** that we have touched it. We must not give in because we have only touched. Whatever **God** has done in the past, His name is still the same.

When hearts are burdened, and they come face to face with the need of the day, they look into **God's** Word. It brings in a propeller of power or the anointing that makes you know He has truly visited. It was a wonderful day when **Jesus** left the glory. I can imagine all the angels, and **God** the **Father** and all heaven so wonderfully stirred that day when the angels were sent to tell that wonderful story.

"Peace on earth and good will to men." It was a glorious day when they beheld the Babe for the first time, and **God** was looking on. What happened after that day and until He was 30 years old I suppose it would take a big book to put it all in. It was working up to a great climax.

I know that Pentecost in my life is working up to a climax; it is not all done in a day. There are many glasses of water and all kinds of times until we get to the real summit of everything. The power of **God** is here to prevail. **God** is with us. The mother of **Jesus** hid a lot of things in her heart.

The time came when it was made manifest at Jordan that **Jesus** was the Son of **God**. Oh, how beautifully it was made known! It had to be made known first to one that was full of the **VISION** of **God**. The **VISION** comes to those who are full. Did it ever strike you we cannot be too full for a **VISION**, we cannot have too much of **God**?

The more of **God**, then the **VISIONS** begin. When **God** has you in His plan, what a change, how things operate. You wonder, you see things in a new light. And how **God** is being glorified as you yield from day to day, and the **Spirit** seems to lay hold of you and bring you on. Yes, it is pressing on, and then He gives us touches of His wonderful power, manifestations of the glory of these things and indications of greater things to follow, and these days which we are living in now speak of better days. How wonderful!

Where should we have been today if we had stopped short if we had not fulfilled the **VISION** which **God** gave us? I am thinking about that time when **Christ** sent the **Spirit**, and Paul did not know much about that; his heart was stirred, his eyes were dim, he was going to put the whole thing to an end in a short time, and **Jesus** was looking on.

We can scarcely understand the whole process only as **God** seems to show us when He gets us into His plan and works with us little by little. We are all amazed that we are amongst the "tongues people;" it is altogether out of order according to the natural. Some of us would have never been in this Pentecostal movement had we not been drawn, but **God** has a wonderful way of drawing us.

 Paul never intended to be among the disciples, Paul never intended to have anything to do with this Man called **Jesus**, but **God** was working, **God** has been working with us and has brought us to this place. It is marvelous! Oh! The **VISION** of **God**, the wonderful manifestation which **God** has for Israel.

I have one purpose in my heart, and it is surely **God's** plan for me, that I want you to see that **Jesus Christ** is the greatest manifestation in all the world, and His power is unequaled, but there is only one way to minister it. I want you to notice that these people after they had seen Paul working wonders by this power, began on a natural line.

 I see it is necessary for me if I want to do anything for **God**, I must get the knowledge of **God**, I must get the **VISION** of **God**, I cannot work on my own. It must be a divine revelation of the Son of **God**. It must be that. I can see as clearly as anything that Paul in his mad pursuit had to be stopped in the way, and after he was stopped in the way and had the **VISION** from heaven and that light from heaven, instantly he realized that he had been working the wrong way.

And as soon as ever the power of the Holy **Ghost** fell upon him; he began in the way in which **God** wanted him to go. And it was wonderful how he had to suffer to come into the way, It is broken spirits, it is tried lives, and it is being driven into a corner as if some strange thing had happened; that is surely the way to get to know the way of **God**.

Paul had not any power to use the name of **Jesus** as he did use it. Only as he had to go through the privations and the difficulties, and even when all things seemed as though shipwrecked, **God** stood by him and made him know that there was something behind all the time that was with him, and able to carry him through, and bring out that for which his heart was all the time longing.

Unconsciously he seemed to be so filled with the **Holy Ghost** that all that was needed was just the bringing of the aprons and the handkerchiefs and sending them forth. I can imagine these people looking on and seeing him and saying, "But it is all in the name, don't you notice that when he sends the handkerchiefs and the aprons he says, 'In the name of the **Lord Jesus** I command that evil to come out.'?"

These people had been looking round and watching, and they thought, "It is only the name, that is all that is needed," and so these men said, "We will do the same." These vagabond Jews, those seven sons of Sceva, were determined to make this thing answer, and they came to the place where that man had been for years possessed with evil power.

As they entered in, they said, "We adjure thee in the name of **Jesus** to come out." The demons said, "**Jesus** we know, and Paul we know, but who are ye?" and this evil power leaped upon them and tore their things off their backs, and they went out naked and wounded.

It was the name; only they did not understand it. Oh, that **God** should help us to understand the name! It is the name, oh! It is still the name, but you must understand there is the ministry of the name, there is something in the name that makes the whole world charmed. It is the **Holy Spirit** back of the ministry, it is the knowledge of Him, it is the ministry of the knowledge of Him, and I can understand it is only that.

I want to speak about the ministry of knowledge; it is important. **God** help us to see. I am satisfied with two things; one is this, I am satisfied it is the knowledge of the Blood of **Jesus Christ** today, and the knowledge of His perfect holiness.

I have been made perfectly cleansed from daming sin. I have been made **Holy** in the knowledge of His holiness. I am satisfied today that as I know Him, the knowledge of His power, that **Christ** is manifested. The power that worketh in me to minister as I am ministering is only in the knowledge of it.

It is effective so that it brings out the very thing which the word of **God** says it will do. The ministry of which, as I know it, it has power over all evil powers by its effectual working in that way. I minister today in the power of the knowledge of the ministry of it, and beyond that, there is a certain sense that I overcome the world according to my faith in Him. I am more than a conqueror over everything just in the knowledge that I have of Him being over everything, as crowned by the **Father** to bring everything into subjection.

Shouting won't do it, but there is lubrication about it which is gloriously felt within and brings it into perfect harmony with the will of **God**. It is not in the shout, and yet we cannot help but shout, but it is in the ministry of the knowledge that He is **Lord** over all demons, all powers of wickedness.

[At this point in the service someone (possibly Wigglesworth) spoke in prophetic tongues. The interpretation was: "The **Holy** One which anointed **Jesus** is so abiding by the **Spirit** in the one that is clothed upon to use the Name till the glory is manifested, and the demons flee, they cannot stand the glory of the manifestation of the **Spirit** which is manifest."]

So I realize that Paul went about clothed in the **Spirit**. This was wonderful. Was his body full of virtue? No! He sent forth handkerchiefs from his body and aprons from his body, and when they touched the needy, they were healed, and demons were cast out. Virtue in his body? No! Virtue in **Jesus**, by the ministry of faith in the name of **Jesus** through the power of the unction of the **Holy Ghost** in Paul.

[Another message in tongues: "The liberty of the **Spirit** bringeth the office."]

It is an office; it is a position; it is a place of rest, of faith. Sometimes the demon powers are dealt with very differently. Not all the same way: but the ministry of the **Spirit** by which it is ministered by the power of the word "**Jesus**." **God** never fails to accomplish the purpose for which the one in charge has wisdom or discernment to see. Along with the **Spirit** of ministry there comes the revelation of the need of the needy one that is bound.

So differently the **Spirit** ministers the name of **Jesus**. I see it continually happening. I see those things answer and all the time the **Lord** is building up a structure of His power by a living faith in the knowledge of the sovereignty of the name of **Jesus**.

If I turn to John's Gospel, I get the whole thing practically in a nutshell. To know Thee, O **God**, and **Jesus Christ** whom Thou hast sent, is eternal life. We must have the knowledge and power of **God** and the knowledge of **Jesus Christ**, the embodiment of **God**, to be clothed upon with **God**, **God** in human flesh.

I see there are those who have come into line. They are possessed with the blessed **Christ** and the power of the Baptism which is the revelation of the **Christ** of **God** within. It is so evidently in the person who is baptized, and that **Christ** is so plainly abiding that the moment he is confronted with evil, instantly he is sensitive of the position of this confronting, and he can deal accordingly.

The difference between the sons of Sceva and Paul is this: They said: "It is only using the word." How many people only use the word, how many times people are defeated because they think it is just the word, how many people have been brokenhearted because it did not answer when they used the word?

"He that believeth shall speak in tongues. He that believeth shall cast out devils, and he that believeth shall lay hands on the sick." To believe is to believe in need of the majesty of the glory of the power, which is all power, which brings all other powers into subjection.

And what is a belief? Sum it up in a few sentences. To believe is to have the knowledge of Him in whom you believe. It is not to believe in the word **Jesus**, but to believe in nature, to believe in the **VISION**, for all power is given unto Him. Greater is He that is within thee in the revelation of faith than he that is in the world.

So I say to you, do not be discouraged if every demon has not gone out. The very moment you have gone, do not think there is an end of it. What we have to do is to see this, that if it had only been using the name, those evil powers would have gone out in that name by the sons of Sceva. It is not that.

It is the virtue of the power of the **Holy Ghost**. It is with the revelation of the Deity of our **Christ** of glory, where all power is given unto Him. In the knowledge of **Christ**, in the faith of what He is, demons must surrender. Demons must go out, and I say it reverently.

God so constructs these bodies of ours that we may be filled with that divine revelation of the Son of **God** till it is manifest to the devils. The Master is in, and they see the Master. **Jesus** I know, and Paul I know. The ministry of the Master! How we need to get to know Him till within us we are fun of the manifestation of the King over all demons.

Brothers and sisters, my heart is full. The depths of my yearnings are for the Pentecostal people. My cry is that we will not miss the opportunity of the Baptism of the **Holy Ghost**, that **Christ** may be manifested in the human till every power of evil will be subject to the **Christ** who is revealed in you, The devils know.

Two important things are before me: To master the situation of myself. You are not going to meet devils if you cannot master yourself, because you soon find the devil bigger than yourself. It is only when you are subdued that **Christ** is enthroned and the embodiment of the **Spirit** is so gloriously covering the human life that **Jesus** is glorified to the full.

So first it is the losing of yourself, and then it is the incoming of another; it is the glorifying of Him which is to fulfill all things, and when He gets lives He can do it. When He gets lives that will so yield themselves to **God**, **God** will be delighted to allow the **Christ** to be so manifested in you, that it will be no difficulty for the devil to know who you are.

I am satisfied that Pentecost is to reestablish **God** in human flesh. Do I need to say it again? The power of the

Holy Ghost has to come to be enthroned in human life, so it does not matter what state we are in. **Christ** is manifested in the place where devils are, the place where religious devils are, the place where a false religion and unbelief is, the place where a formal religion has taken the place of holiness and righteousness.

You have to need to be living in holiness and living in the righteousness, and **Spirit** of the Master so that in every walk of life everything that is not like our **Lord Jesus** will have to depart and that is what is needed today. I ask you in the **Holy Ghost** to seek the place where He is in power.

"**Jesus** I know, Paul I know but who are ye?" May **God** stamp it upon us for the devil is not afraid of you. May the **Holy Ghost** makes us today terrors of evil doers, for the **Holy Ghost** came into us to judge the world of sin, of unbelief, of righteousness, and that is the purpose of the **Holy Ghost**. The devils will know us, and **Jesus** will know us.

Ezekiel's VISION of dry bones

I want to turn to a portion of the Old Testament scriptures, 37th chapter of Ezekiel. I want you to see in this particularly situation, how a man was so full of the **Spirit**, was so deep in the **Spirit** that the hand of the **Lord** was upon him, and he was being led in the **Spirit**. He was in a place of rest, and power. I want you to keep this thought before you. He had come to a place where he could rest in **God**, and where he knew **God** was with him, and that he could live there. This is a very important truth.

Some people have an idea that they have to be doing some activity every moment to get results. I beseech you, by the power of the **Holy Ghost** today, that you see that there is only one thing that is going to accomplish the purposes of **God**, and that is being in the **Spirit**. I don't care how dry the land is; I don't care how thirsty the land is, or how many vessels or how few there are around about; I beseech you, in the name of **Jesus**, that you keep in the **Spirit**. That's the secret.

Here is a man who was in the right place, at the right time, and **God** does know it. **"The Lord knoweth them that are his."** [2Ti 2.19] **Ezekiel said:**

"The Lord carried me out in the Spirit, and set me down in the midst of the valley, which was full of dry bones; and caused me to pass by them round about; and, behold, there were very many in the open valley; and, lo, they were very dry. And he said unto me, 'Son of man, can these bones live?' And I answered, 'O Lord God, thou knowest.'" [Ek 37.1-3]

The **VISION** is the **Lord**'s, and you can see the **Lord**'s **VISION** only by being in the **Spirit**. When you are in the **Spirit** and dry bones are around about you and barren conditions are all about you, You think everything is exactly opposite to what you desire. You can see no deliverance by human power, and then knowing that your condition is known to **God**.

God is looking for men and women who are willing to submit, and submit, and SUBMIT, and yield, and yield, and YIELD to the **Holy Spirit** until their bodies are saturated and soaked with **God**; you realize that **God** your **Father** has you in such condition that at any moment he can reveal his will to you and communicate whatever He wants to say to you. **"Can these bones live?" "Thou knowest, O Lord."** "Yes, I know. What do you think?" "From what I have known of you, blessed Master, in the past, I believe that these dry bones can live, for you say so." "Very true, my child, go and prophesy. Do as I tell you."

Now I want you to understand that there is something more to this. I want you to see that **God** is everything to us. I believe that we have to come to a place where we have to submit ourselves to the mighty power of **God**. Where we shall see we are in the perfect will of **God**. I pray **God** that the **Holy Ghost** will show us our leanness, our farness from this **Holy** place. What **God** wants in us is a great hunger and thirst for this place.

He said, **"O ye dry bones, hear the word of the Lord." [Ek 37.4]** I would like you to understand that **God** speaks first, and he speaks so loud and so clear and so distinct that this man (who was filled with the **Spirit** of the **Lord**) heard every word.

 Still, there is not any movement in this dead, dry valley until the word of the **Lord** is spoken. The bones are dry, very dry and dead. But what does is it matter? **God** has spoken, and the WORD has gone forth. What is it that is spoken? Ah, it is only that the word of **God** has gone forth through his servant the prophet.

The world has to be brought to a knowledge of the truth, but that will only be brought about through human instruments, and that will be when human instruments are at a place where they will say with all of their hearts: I will only say that which the **Holy Ghost** directs me to say!

Ezekiel rose up, clothed with the divine power. He began to speak, he began to prophesy; and then as soon as he began to speak there was a mighty rattling among the bones, [Ek 37.7] If we had been there, we should have seen a bigger stir than we had ever seen before. Bone to bone at the voice of a man filled with the **Spirit** of the living **God**. **God** had given him victory over utter and complete death. So **God** in like manner wants to give to each of us total victory in every situation.

What does the word say? **"Be still, and know that I am God" [Ps 46.10]** It is a place of complete tranquility where we know, that we know that **God** is controlling and moving us by the mighty power of his **Spirit**.

Beloved that is a place which we can reach. This prophecy is for us. Truly **God** wants to begin this in us. We must always remember that it is **God** who is the creator, and his creative power is at work at this very moment. **God** knows where there is barrenness and where there is thirsty land, and it is He who can bring forth springs of living water.

There are many dry places. Indeed, nearly every town I go to is said to be the driest of places—"the hardest town in the kingdom," they will say. What is that to do with you? The **Lord**'s hand is not shortened that it cannot save. [Is 59.1] It is in man's extremity that **God** finds his greatest opportunity. It is for his word to awaken his beloved church, and so **God** wants us with great hope!

"All things are possible to them that believe." [Mk 9.23] But if we are to do the will of **God** at the right time and the right place, we must yield to the **Spirit** and obey him in every situation, to give **God** an opportunity to work in and through us. **Philippians 2:13 For it is God which worketh in you both to will and to do of his good pleasure.**

"And I prophesied as was commanded." [Ek 37.7] He just did what he was told to do. It takes more to live in that place than in any other place that I know of—to live in a place where you hear **God's** voice and obey. It is only by the power of the **Holy Spirit** that you can do as you are told quickly and without resistance.

"And as I prophesied there was a noise, and behold, a shaking, and the bones came together, bone to his bone." [Ek 37.7] There is something worth your recognition in this. It is only the **Spirit** that can make the crooked straight, raise the dead, and perform miracles.

Some of you, no doubt, have thought some of your neighbors are a bit crooked and were, in fact, some of the most crooked of-the-way bones you ever saw in your life, and it would be impossible for them to get saved.

That is nothing to do with you. It is for you to live in the **Holy Ghost**, and he can change the whole circumstance, and you will be amazed at the way the crooked bones will be straightened. Nothing can change such circumstances as **God** can.

"Bone to bone," no crooked places now; but it takes **God** to do that. Man has been trying to do it all along, but as soon as a man has been truly baptized with the **Holy Ghost**, **God** does it. There is power in the **Holy Ghost** to transform, renew, and change the whole circumstances of life. You have to submit and let **God** take hold of you. Don't be troubled because you have not reached the place. You have reached somewhere, but the best is in store. Only yield so that he may have full control of all you are.

"And when I beheld, lo, the sinews and flesh came upon them, and the skin covered them above, but there was no breath in them." [Ek 37.8] Here's a condition for them. There was the form, but no breath in it. But you must never give in and think the thing is fairly accomplished if you see the joining of the members and a kind of fellowship.

You must never give in with that. They are never in the royal place until the breath of **God** has come into them and upon them. You must always lead people to receive the **Holy Ghost** and know that the breath of the Almighty is upon them. Justification will not be sufficient to accomplish the purpose of **God**. They may be justified and sanctified, but can never be satisfied until they are filled with the **Holy Ghost**.

There must be a real travailing of the human heart for **God** to bring forth. People are never safe until they are baptized with the **Holy Ghost**, and that is why the apostles pressed that fact upon believers, and that is why **Jesus** was always pointing to the time when they should be filled with unction and power of the **Spirit** which would carry them all on.

"Then said he unto me: Prophesy… So I prophesied." [Ek 37.9-10] Glory to **God**! It is most wonderful. As soon as he began to prophesy he found there was something in it. Are you not wanting to get there? Don't you think we ought to be there? Do you think we ought to be satisfied until we are there? How can **God** be pleased with us until we reach that place? We must get to that place where we shall see **God** and know his voice when he sends us with a message that brings life and power and victory. "And they stood up upon their feet, an exceeding great army." [Ek 39.10]

I know a lot of people who are seeking their baptism in a wonderful way. They see **VISIONS**, and it is scriptural that they should see **VISIONS**. I believe that Paul was so imbued with the **Holy Ghost** and so filled with the glory of **God** that he could at times see **VISIONS** and revelations.

John in the **Spirit**. I want to point out something. John the divine preached all over the country, and the enemies of **Christ** gnashed upon him with their teeth, and they tried to the best of their power to destroy him. Tradition says that they even put him in a pot of boiling oil, but, like a cat, he seemed to have nine lives, I tell you there is something in the power of the **Holy Spirit**.

When **God** wants to keep a man, nothing can destroy him. My life is in the hands of **God**. What can separate us from the love of **God**? Can heights or depths? [Ro 8.39] Is there anything that can separate us? No, praise **God**! Nothing can separate us.

No, his enemies said they could not kill him, so they cast him away on the rocky and desolate island of Patmos. They thought that would be an end of him; and there, on that lonely isle, he was "in the **Spirit**." [Rv 1.10] Have you ever been there?" The very place that was not fit for humanity was the place where he was most filled with **God**, and where he was most ready for the revelation of **Jesus**.

Oh, beloved, I tell you there is something in the baptism in the **Holy Ghost** worthy of our whole attention, worthy of our whole consideration in every way. The baptism in the **Holy Ghost**! Yes, the barren wilderness, the rocky and desolate isle, the dry land, and the most unfriendly place, may be filled with **God**.

You read the first chapter of the Revelation, and you will see that in the 9th and 10th verses that John was in the **Spirit** on the **Lord**'s Day, and behind him a great voice as of a trumpet. [Rv 1.9-10] Immediately a revelation was made to him, which you cannot read without being blessed. The revelation given to him was a series of **Holy** truths that have yet to be fulfilled and will be fulfilled to the letter. There are wonderful things there. Blessed be **God**, we can come to that place which he speaks about. **Jesus** can reveal His mind to us from time to time.

If you only think about it, you will see you are in a thousand times better position than John. In that barren place, he was filled with the **Spirit**. You can have no excuse, for the lines have fallen to you in pleasant places. You will see from the second verse of the 4th chapter of Revelation that John was in so living and blessed a condition of fellowship with **God** that immediately he was "in the **Spirit**." [Rv 4.2]

Immediately! What does it mean? It means this: That **God** wants us to be in a place where the least breath of heaven makes us all on **FIRE**, ready for everything. You say, "How can I have that?" Oh, you can have that as easy as anything. "Can I?" Yes, it is as simple as possible. "How?"

Let heaven come in; let the **Holy Ghost** takes possession of you, and when he comes into your body you will find out that that is the keynote of the **Spirit** of joy and the **Spirit** of rapture, and if you allow the **Holy Ghost** to have full control you will find you are living in the **Spirit**, and you will find out that the opportunities will be **God's** opportunities, and there is a difference between **God's** opportunities and ours. You will find you have come to the right place at the right time, and you will speak the right word at the right time and in the right place, and you will not go a warfare at your charge.

How to Live in the Miraculous!

This is a quick explanation of how to live and move in the realm of the miraculous. Seeing divine interventions of **God** is not something that just spontaneously happens because you have been born-again. There are certain biblical principles and truths that must be evident in your life. This is a very basic list of some of these truths and laws:

1. You must give **Jesus Christ** your whole heart. You cannot be lackadaisical in this endeavour. Being lukewarm in your walk with **God** is repulsive to the **Lord**. He wants 100% commitment. **Jesus** gave His all, now it is our turn to give our all. He loved us 100%. Now we must love Him 100%.

My son, give me thine heart, and let thine eyes observe my ways (Proverbs 23:26).

So then because thou art lukewarm, and neither cold nor hot, I will spew thee out of my mouth (Revelation 3:16).

2. There must be a complete agreement with **God's** Word. We must be in harmony with the **Lord** in our attitude, actions, thoughts, and deeds. Whatever the Word of **God** declares in the New Testament is what we wholeheartedly agree with.

Can two walk together, except they be agreed? (Amos 3:3).

For the eyes of the LORD run to and fro throughout the whole earth, to shew himself strong in the behalf of them whose heart is perfect toward him (2 Chronicles 16:9).

3. Obey and do the Word from the heart, from the simplest to the most complicated request or command. No matter what the

Word says to do, do it! Here are some simple examples: Lift your hands in praise, in everything give thanks, forgive instantly, gather together with the saints, and give offerings to the **Lord**, and so on.

I can of mine own self do nothing: as I hear, I judge: and my judgment is just; because I seek not mine own will, but the will of the Father which hath sent me (John 5:30).

4. Make **Jesus** the highest priority of your life. Everything you do, do not do it as unto men, but do it as unto **God**.

If ye then be risen with Christ, seek those things which are above, where Christ sitteth on the right hand of God. Set your affection on things above, not on things on the earth (Colossians 3:1-2).

5. Die to self! The old man says, "My will be done!" The new man says, "**God's** will be done!"

I am crucified with Christ: nevertheless I live; yet not I, but Christ liveth in me: and the life which I now live in the flesh I live by the faith of the Son of God, who loved me, and gave himself for me (Galatians 2:20).

Now if we be dead with Christ, we believe that we shall also live with him (Romans 6:8).

6. Repent the minute you get out of **God's** will—no matter how minor, or small the sin may seem.

Revelation 3:19 As many as I love, I rebuke and chasten: be zealous therefore, and repent.

7. Take one step at a time. **God** will test you (not to do evil) to see if you will obey him. *Whatever He tells you to do: by His Word, by His **Spirit**, or within your conscience, do it.* He will never tell you to do something contrary to His nature or His Word!

For whosoever shall do the will of my Father which is in

heaven, the same is my brother, and sister, and mother (Matthew 12:50).

ABOUT THE AUTHOR

Michael met and married his Wonderful wife (Kathleen) in 1978. As a direct result of the Author and his wife's personal, amazing experiences with God, they have had the privilege to serve as pastors/apostles, missionaries, evangelist, broadcasters, and authors for over four decades. By Gods Divine enablement's and Grace, Doc Yeager has written over 175 books, ministered over 10,000 Sermons, and having helped to start over 25 churches. His books are filled with hundreds of their amazing testimonies of Gods protection, provision, healing's, miracles, and answered prayers. They flow in the gifts of the Holy Spirit, teaching the word of God, Wonderful signs following and confirming God's word. Websites Connected to Doc Yeager.

www.docyeager.com

www.jilmi.org

www.wbntv.org

<u>Some of the Books Written by Doc Yeager:</u>

"Living in the Realm of the Miraculous – "1 to 5 "
"I need God Cause I'm Stupid"
"The Miracles of Smith Wigglesworth"
"How Faith Comes 28 WAYS"
"Horrors of Hell, Splendors of Heaven"
"The Coming Great Awakening"
"Sinners in The Hands of an Angry GOD",
"Brain Parasite Epidemic"
"My JOURNEY to HELL" - illustrated for teenagers
"Divine Revelation of Jesus Christ"
"My Daily Meditations"
"Holy Bible of JESUS CHRIST"
"War In The Heavenlies - (Chronicles of Micah)"
"My Legal Rights to Witness"
"Why We (MUST) Gather! - 30 Biblical Reasons"
"My Incredible, Supernatural, Divine Experiences"
"How GOD Leads & Guides! - 20 Ways"
"Weapons of Our Warfare"
"How You Can Be Healed"
"Hell Is For Real"
"Heaven Is For Real"
"God Still Heals"
"God Still Provides"
"God Still Protects"
"God Still Gives Dreams & Visions"
"God Still Does Miracles"
"God Still Gives Prophetic Words"
"Life Changing Quotes of Smith Wigglesworth"